WISDOM
Through
Character Development

A Pedagogical Guide to Worship in Schools

Rita Henriquez-Green, EdD
and
William H. Green, PhD

Order this book online at www.trafford.com
or email orders@trafford.com

Most Trafford titles are also available at major online book retailers.

Printed in the United States of America.

ISBN: 978-1-4669-5122-8 (sc)

Trafford rev. 11/15/2012

 www.trafford.com

North America & international
toll-free: 1 888 232 4444 (USA & Canada)
phone: 250 383 6864 ♦ fax: 812 355 4082

Introduction

If I could give you a written guarantee today that you would never fail as a school teacher, or that all your students would be successful, how many of you would be interested in taking the advice?

In 2 Peter 1: 4-10 we find God's scriptural instructions on the way schools should be run academically. God never once said the most important thing you are to do as a teacher is to teach knowledge. That is the third most important on God's list. The first thing God says we need to teach is faith. The second is virtue and the third is knowledge. In Genesis 2: 16, 17, God talks about two trees. What are they? They are the Tree of Life and the Tree of Knowledge of Good and Evil. God told Adam and Eve they could freely eat of any tree except the Tree of Knowledge of Good and Evil. God said, "I do not want you to have knowledge of good and evil." You know that has never changed. God still doesn't want us to know good and evil. He wants us to go to Him, the Tree of Life, and allow him to tell us what's good and evil.

People who work for the Unites States Department of Treasury never see counterfeit money. They deal with the real thing every day as they've been trained over and over and over again. When they are working at banks, they can find a counterfeit bill the instant they touch it. Why? Because they've dealt with the real thing so much anything that's counterfeit stands out immediately. That's the way God wants us to be and to train our students. They will not have to try out drugs, etc., to find out whether they are right or wrong.

Let's go back to 2 Peter. Years ago God was taken out of our nation's public school system; that was the elimination of faith, the first on the list. So we start with step two, virtue. What is virtue? One definition is "The quality of doing what is right and avoiding what is wrong." The Bible is our guide to virtue. The teachers said, "We don't have God or the Bible, but we still want you to mind, behave, and do right." The students' response was, "Why?"

In 1976, the valedictorian for Yale University, a very prestigious school by the world's standards, stood up for his address and said, "Ladies and gentlemen of the faculty, you have given me and my fellow students the greatest education money can buy in this world today, but you never told us why," and he sat down. The students gave him a ten minute standing ovation.

I don't think there is anyone who is reading this that would disagree with me if I said that the most important thing that could happen to a person is to come to know the Lord as his/ her Savior. That is # 1 on the list. God says there's a second most important thing that can happen in your life and that is to know how to live your life, to know what life is all about; it is to know how to develop proper character. He warns us in Genesis not to go for knowledge, and what does the wisest man that ever lived say in Proverbs 4:5-7? He doesn't say get knowledge, he says get wisdom, and wisdom comes through gaining virtue, and we can attain virtue through character development.

As you plan your classes, I challenge you not to zero in on knowledge, but to zero in on virtue, or character building, and knowledge will follow. There is no doubt in my mind that this one principle will change your teaching.

If you are not doing this right now, don't get discouraged. Remember that the real art of living is beginning where you are and that "where you stand is not important, it is in what direction you are moving that counts (Oliver Wendell Holmes).

After teaching for many years in elementary schools, high schools and college, I know that proper character does make a difference. I'm sharing the following worships which have made a difference in my class and in my students' lives.

The following is a suggested introduction for the class:

> Good morning. This semester we are going to do something different for worship. Can anyone define character or explain what it is? After you have thought about it, Turn-to-your-neighbor and tell what you think character means. The definition we will use is "Character is the way in which a person feels, thinks, and acts." In the Bible, God tells us how we should feel, think, and act. We are going to study one character trait for two weeks. We are going to learn what it means. We will read about people who have developed this specific character trait and how it has helped them. Most important of all, we'll find out what God says about it. Then we will work on developing this trait in our lives and in everything we do. As a class, let us discover how Mom and Dad (family) and our friends feel about the results. If you are really serious, you will be surprised because everyone will notice the difference.

Teacher: For maximum effectiveness, some method should be devised for students to accumulate their written work. Each Friday, the student is to write the definition, text, a recap of his or her favorite story, and a personal experience involving the trait for that week. Examples for collecting the written work could include folders, notebooks, electronic notebooks, portfolios, Wiki's, web sites, etc.)

The following contains an overview of the weekly schedule.

Weekly Schedule

Week 1:

Monday:	Introduce word and share weekend happenings or read a story.
Tuesday:	Students learn definition. Tell story # 2.
Wednesday:	Learn text. Tell story.
Thursday:	Complete recitation of definition and text. Read the next story.
Friday:	Perfect recitation. Special activity. Use Story Hour CD's or MP3 files, (http://www.yourstoryhour.org/transaction.php) share personal experience. Write definition and text, recap his/her favorite story under stories, and a personal experience. Page four shows how the students' notebooks can be set up. The students can also use pages from *A Reason for Handwriting* (See textbook list from your Union) to write the definition or text. They can decorate these and share with others either by hard copy or by electronic posting.

Week 2: The following teaching structures are featured

Monday:	T-chart
Tuesday:	Four Corners
Wednesday:	Ranking
Thursday:	Either/Or
Friday:	Teachers have a variety of activities they can use to keep students engaged and excited about developing their character.

Table of Contents

With special thanks to Betty Chapin, Kathy Couch, Barbara Moore, and the Carolina Conference for their encouragement, support, and hard work.

DEDICATION

To Mom and Dad, who mean so much to me, who have always stood for the right and have encouraged, influenced, and inspired me; and to my husband, William, for his willingness to share his wisdom and expertise.

Week One & Two

Table of Contents

Week One

Week Two

Perseverance

Perseverance

- Introduction
  - Definition
  - Text
  - Stories
  - My Experiences
- Perseverance Teaching Procedure
  - Monday
  - Tuesday
  - Wednesday
  - Thursday
  - Friday
- Perseverance Stories
  - Brenda's Skates
  - The Rabbit and the Turtle
  - Helen Succeeds
  - You Can Be Anything
  - Never Give Up

Teacher: Find a permanent place on the chalkboard, whiteboard, or transparency for Worship. Arrange the following information on the chalkboard, whiteboard, or transparency:

Perseverance

Definition:	Continuing to do something in spite of difficulties or obstacles. (For younger students you may use "finishing up a job even when it is hard.")
Attributes:	(1) You have a difficult task to complete; (2) You want to give up; (3) You continue working on it patiently until the task is completed.
Text:	Matthew 19:26—"With God all things are possible."*
Stories:	At the end of the week you may ask students to write about their favorite story/object lesson from those shared during the week.
My Experiences:	Students write about a personal experience involving the trait for the week. Students may take pictures and post, interview someone and post, prepare a short video, or other media enhanced method to present their experience.

You could also make a digital record of the word, definition, attributes, text, stories, and my experience and post it on the class webpage, wiki, or electronic notebook. However, it is imperative that you create a specific place for worship where students can see the information throughout the day.

* You may use another appropriate text if you choose.

Perseverance Teaching Procedure Week 1

Monday

"Turn-to-your-neighbor and tell them what the word is for this week. That's correct. The word is **perseverance**. Let's all repeat it together using a complete sentence. Good job. Let's read together the meaning of the word **perseverance** using a complete sentence." (**Perseverance** means continuing to do something in spite of difficulties or obstacles.) "Very good. Turn-to-your-neighbor and repeat the meaning of the word **perseverance**. Excellent!

"The text in the Bible that encourages us to be persevering is Matthew 19:26**—'With God all things are possible.' Now, turn to a different neighbor at your table and tell them the text in the Bible that encourages us to be **persevering**. Remember, use a complete sentence. The text in the Bible that encourages us to be **persevering** is Matthew 19:26—'With God all things are possible.' Fantastic. Let's all say it together." (Teacher—have the students use complete sentences.)

Talk about the weekend or read "Brenda's Skates" story. (P.10)

Pray: "When we pray, let's ask God to help us not to give up, but to be **persevering**."

Tuesday

"Good morning, class! Use a complete sentence to tell your neighbor the word we are studying this week" (Reply—"The word we are studying this week is **perseverance**.") "Very good. Now use a complete sentence to repeat the definition of **perseverance** to a different neighbor at your table." (I like the way Patrice is turning to another neighbor to give the definition.)

"This morning I'm going to give the class two minutes to memorize the word and definition. Then each of you will be able to recite it all by yourself. After one minute, you may practice with a neighbor. I will let you know when you have one minute left. Ready, start memorizing." (If you have not done so yet, remember to model and review tips for memorizing. Give them two minutes and then you may want to begin.) "I will go first. The word we are studying this week is **perseverance**. **Perseverance** means continuing to do something in spite of difficulties or obstacles."

After two minutes say "Who is ready?" (Give everyone a chance. Ask those who you know will be able to repeat it easily to go first. As you use these worships, you will notice the students' memory will improve even with their regular class work.)

"All of you did such a good job. Let's all say it together." (Reply—"The word we are studying this week is **perseverance**. **Perseverance** means continuing to do something in spite of difficulties or obstacles.")

Read: "The Rabbit and Turtle" story. (p. 11)

Use Think-square-share to identify examples of **perseverance** in the story. The recorder will write and the reporter will report. Make sure the social skills person gets all group members involved in squaring. Make sure that each of the four people in the group contributes at least one idea.

Call on different tables to report—they can each give one example and then open the floor.

Think-pair-square-share—"How can you be **persevering** right here in the classroom?" Use Random Call cards to share responses.

"Your assignment is to observe when your classmates or you are practicing **perseverance**. We will talk about it again tomorrow."

Challenge students: "I want you to find some way of being **persevering** at home this week. Be ready to share it with us on Friday." (TEACHER: Don't be afraid to use personal examples. They need a model. Example—this morning I was **persevering** because even though I didn't want to prepare breakfast, I did without giving up.)

Pray: Remind students to include the character trait (**perseverance**) they are working on.

Wednesday

"Good morning, class. This morning, let's say the word and the definition of the word we have been studying without looking at the board. Let's try it. Remember, we must use a complete sentence." (Reply—"The word we are studying this week is **perseverance**, and the definition of the word **perseverance** is continuing to do something in spite of difficulties or obstacles.") "Excellent. Many said it without looking at the board."

"Today, it's going to be harder. But since the verse is so simple I'm only going to give you one minute to learn the verse. Remember you must use a complete sentence." You'll need to say, "The text in the Bible that helps us to be **persevering** is Matthew 19:26—'With God, all things are possible.'"

"Think for 1 minute. I will tell you when your minute is up. Ready, Start. Now Turn-to-your-neighbor to practice the verse." Give them 15-30 seconds.

"Who is ready? I see many hands." (Randomly call on one student. Let everyone try and give them all positive reinforcement. Remember the praise needs to be specific. For example, Ronnie, you were able to say the verse quickly and without any errors. Good work.)

Read: "Helen Succeeds" story (p.12).

Ask Questions:

Use Think-pair-share. Use Random Call cards.

1. Who is persevering in this story? (Literal, Knowledge)
2. In what ways was he/she/ or they persevering? (Comprehension)
3. Have any of you been persevering? In what ways? (Application, Analysis)

Pray: Always include something about **perseverance**.

Teacher: During the day, comment on those who are **persevering**. "Steve is practicing **perseverance**. Although he had a hard time with a math problem, he redid it without complaining and succeeded. Good for you, Steve! George is not giving up; he is recopying his writing neatly."

Thursday

"Good morning, class! Today is the day we are trying to say the word, the definition, and the text all without looking. Let me try. The word for this week is **perseverance**. **Perseverance** is continuing to do something in spite of difficulties or obstacles, and the text in the Bible that encourages us to be **persevering** is Matthew 19:26—'With God all things are possible.'

"I'll give you three minutes." (Change the amount of time as needed.) "After two minutes, you may practice with a neighbor. Who is ready to say it just as I did?" Let everyone try. Those who have difficulty, say, "You are doing it well and just need to study it a little bit more. I'll give you another chance tomorrow. Don't give up." At the beginning some may have problems, but by the third week it seems easy for all and they love it. Be sure to give lots of specific positive reinforcement. "I can't believe so many of you know the word, definition, and text word for word and can say it without making one error. That's excellent," etc.

(When people visit, show what the students can do. The students enjoy doing it and it is impressive. Remember to take every opportunity to use the word and comment on it.)

Read: "You Can Be Anything" story. (p. 14)

Use a Think-square-share to answer the following questions:

1. Who was persevering in this story? (Literal, Knowledge)
2. How was the person persevering? (Comprehension)
3. How can perseverance help you be a better student? (Creative, Synthesis)
4. Who has noticed a classmate who has been persevering? Be sure to include in what ways they were persevering. (Application, Analysis)

"Let's keep working on **perseverance** all through the day." Give some examples yourself. You need to be sure to include everyone.

Pray: Always include something about **perseverance**.

Friday

"Good morning, class!" Do something special on this day. Begin with the story "Never Give Up!" or another special activity or invite a visitor to make a special presentation. This may be one way to involve the pastors from the different churches. If you do have the pastor or another visitor come, have the students show what they have learned first.

Repeat the word, definition, and text all together. Anyone who did not say it the day before let him or her try now. If you have a visitor, have different students recite the different parts. Praise them all for their specific responses.

"Today all of you need to show me where you have written the word, text, definition, stories, and your experience on paper just as I have it on the board. Under stories, write one of the stories you remember that we discussed this week, telling how the person was persevering" (Knowledge, Comprehension). "Under experience, write what you did to be persevering here or at home" (Application). "You may also write the definition and text on another piece of paper and decorate it" (Knowledge, Creativity). "You could give this to one of your parents or another teacher. Who else might enjoy these?" (The list can include school staff, lay church members, parents, etc.)

Students may begin writing on their notebooks/portfolios, as early as Monday but save the decorating of the paper for Friday. You just want them to make a notebook or portfolio. These may be either paper or ink or electronic. Be sure they keep a list of the words so they can review them later.

Special Note: Make this day special. Be creative!!!!!

Stories of Perseverance

Brenda's Skates

If there was one thing more than another that Brenda wanted for her birthday, it was a pair of roller skates. How she coaxed and coaxed for them! How she promised to be as good as gold for the next ten years if only Mother or Father would give her a pair!

In vain her mother explained that Brenda might not learn to use them as easily as other children, that she might fall many times and perhaps hurt herself before she could skate properly. Brenda wanted the skates and that was that.

She thought about skates all day and dreamed about skates all night. She pictured herself skating to school and home again, skating to the stores for Mother, and skating all over the yard, of course. Was her birthday never going to come?

It came at last, and with it the precious parcel for which she had longed. Somehow, even before she opened it, she guessed there were skates inside. And there were. Beautiful, new, shiny skates. Just her size, too. What bliss! Brenda felt she had never been so happy in all her life.

And now to practice with them. Scarcely was breakfast over before she was out on the smooth concrete in front of the garage, strapping on the skates. At last, she thought, I am going to skate!

Eagerly she stood up. But only for a moment. Suddenly, to her great surprise, away went both her feet from under her. Down she went. Bang! "Mother!" she cried. "That hurt."

But Mother was indoors and did not notice. So Brenda stood up again. But hardly had she put one foot forward, when the other, for some reason, started running backward and down she went again, this time on her face.

Bang! This really hurt, and Brenda felt very much like crying. Slowly she got up once more and started to walk. But before she knew what was happening, bang! She was sitting on the concrete again.

Somehow she just couldn't do it. Up she got and down she went. It was a case of bump, bump, bump, and bang, bang, bang, until certain parts of her were quiet sore. And she felt very sad. All her hopes of skating to school and to town like the other girls faded away.

As she sat on the concrete again, tears filled her eyes. She began to wish she had never asked for skates for her birthday. Why hadn't she asked for a new doll? Or a new baby carriage? She wouldn't have gotten hurt then.

"What's the matter?" called Mother. "Tired of skating already?"

"No," said Brenda crossly. "But I can't skate. I've fallen down so often I'm sore all over." "Don't give up yet," said Mother. "You haven't started to learn. You must keep on trying till you succeed."

"Trying!" cried Brenda. "I've tried all I'm going to. I tell you, Mother, I'm sore. Sore! And I wish I had never asked for skates."

"Oh, tut, tut!" said Mother. "You are giving up altogether too easily." "So would you," said Brenda, "if you had fallen on the same place as many times as I have this morning. Skating is not for me."

"But, Brenda," said Mother, "you are not going to let the other girls beat you, are you?" "I don't care," said Brenda. "I can't skate. I just can't. So there!"

"You mustn't say can't," said Mother. "You can. But while skating comes easily to some, it is very hard for others. Why, I don't know. Once I saw two children get skates for the first time. One put them on and sailed away just as if she had skated all her life. The other fell all over the place. But she tried and tried and tried again, until now she can skate as well as anybody else."

"Do you think I could do it, too, if I tried?" asked Brenda. "Of course," said Mother. "And I'll come along and help you." "Now?" "Yes, now," said Mother. So on went the skates once more, and down went Brenda on the same sore spot. But she got up again and, leaning on Mother, went carefully forward.

Slowly, gradually, she got the idea of how to do it, how to balance herself, how to swing her weight gently, easily, this way and that. Now and then, when all seemed to go wrong and she was sprawled all over the concrete, she wanted to give up and throw the skates away, but Mother would insist on her keeping going.

"You must never even think you can't do it," she said. "Just keep on trying, trying, trying, no matter how many times you fall. It's just like learning to do any difficult task in life. Never give up. Keep trying till you win."

So Brenda tried and tried again. Several days later she was skating round the concrete all by herself. Soon she was out on the sidewalk with the other girls, skating to school. By trying and trying and "sticking it out" she made her dream come true.

From *Uncle Arthur's Bedtime Stories*
by permission of Review and Herald

The Rabbit and The Turtle

One day a turtle was creeping down the road. A rabbit came hopping along.

"Good morning, Mr. Turtle," said the rabbit. "Don't you wish you could run as fast as I can?"

"You run fast and I go slowly," said the turtle. "But I think I can beat you in a race."

"What!" said the rabbit. "You, beat me in a race! I can go ten times as fast as you can."

"Yes," said the rabbit, "but I am foolish to run with an old creeper like you. Where shall we race?"

"Let us go from this big tree to the big tree by the river," said the turtle. "We will start when you count to three."

"One, two, three—go!" Said the rabbit.

Away he ran as fast as he could go.

He ran a little way, and then he looked back. The turtle was not in sight.

"I will stop and eat some of these green leaves," said the rabbit. "Then I will run on to the tree."

So he stopped and ate the green leaves. Then he said, "That old creeper is not in sight. I will lie down awhile and rest. Then I will run to the big tree by the river. I shall be there long before Mr. Turtle comes."

So the rabbit lay down, and soon he was fast asleep. When he woke up, he looked back. He did not see the turtle. "I may as well go on," he said.

He ran to the big tree by the river. There under the tree sat the turtle! The turtle was slow, but he did not stop until he had reached the end of the race. And that is how he won.

Aesop's Fables

Helen Succeeds

B aby Helen bounced and cooed, and filled the nursery with laughter. When she heard the birds sing, she turned her head and smiled. She liked to poke her nose into the heart of a rose and feel its petals tickle her face. She touched the flowers softly as she looked at their delicate colors and smelled their perfume. Her bright eyes didn't miss a thing. She was quick and intelligent and lively. Father and Mother Keller were proud of their daughter.

For almost two years little Helen brought joy and sunshine to the Keller household. And then one day she became very ill. The doctors could do nothing for her. They didn't expect her to live.

She did live, however. But the burning fever left her without sight or hearing. She had become both blind and deaf and because she couldn't hear, she didn't learn to talk as other children do.

The little girl who had loved to look at the flowers and listen to the sounds of nature was suddenly plunged into a dark, silent world.

Happy little Helen changed. Because she couldn't understand what had happened, she became bad-tempered and contrary. She wouldn't let anyone comb her hair or straighten her clothing.

Then Mother and Father brought a special teacher into their home to teach their handicapped daughter a new kind of language. The teacher made words with her finger tips in Helen's hand. After much practice, Helen began to "talk" in this way. She learned to "see" by feeling the plants and animals that she had loved so much. The rabbits, squirrels, frogs, and grasshoppers became her friends again. The buttercups, the wild-flowers, and the leaves on the trees once more brought smiles to her face.

Life became a school. Helen wanted to learn the names of everything she touched. Questions, questions, questions. She once again became delighted with the world about her. She quickly learned to read and write in Braille, the printed language for the blind.

Soon Helen went to a special school for the blind and deaf, with her patient teacher-friend always by her side to "write" in her hand. She surprised her teachers by learning very rapidly. She worked hard and soon graduated from this school.

Helen was determined to learn to talk with her mouth. Although it was considered impossible for a deaf-blind person to learn to do so, Helen did learn to speak quite well. But it took much effort and hard work with her patient teacher.

Helen now surprised everyone by saying she wanted to go to college—a college for seeing and hearing students. She chose a very famous school, and graduated with highest honors. Her teacher-friend, whom she had learned to love with all her heart, sat by her side during classes and "wrote" into her hand.

To Helen Keller, the word IMPOSSIBLE meant "do it". She accomplished many things with more skill than lots of people who could see and hear. She learned to read and write many languages. She learned to love God and people. She went all over the world making speeches to interest people in helping the blind and deaf. As a result, schools were established particularly for these people. She became a good writer and many of her articles were published in famous magazines.

Although Helen couldn't see or hear, she didn't give up. She used her other senses—touch, taste, and smell—to reopen the wonderful world to her understanding. She spent her life in serving others. She became a truly great woman, in spite of her handicaps.

From *Living and Learning* by Sadie Engen
by permission of Review and Herald

You Can Be Anything

If someone had told me nine years ago that I would have written a junior devotional someday, I would have laughed out loud and kept on laughing through the night. Because nine years ago I was not a writer. I had stories in my head that I wanted to share, but I thought no one would want to hear what I had to say. I thought that somewhere there was a group of "chosen" people who did all the writing, and since no one had asked me if I wanted to be a part of them, I couldn't expect to join their ranks.

Then one day I sent a two-page story to "Our Little Friend," and they bought it! What elation! And a whole $7! Next I decided to try writing a book. I wrote down my outline and two chapters and mailed them to an Adventist publisher. The editor wrote back, asking to see the whole thing.

Two and a half years later, after rewrites and additions and numerous mailings back and forth, that book became "No More Alphabet Soup." With more than a little discomfort, I endured the family's bantering about how they finally had an author in the family. But I felt no different inside than before I'd written my book. I also knew that having a book published didn't mean I was a better writer than anyone else.

Other people can tell a story better than I can. Some of them do it, and others just dream. Maybe you are one of the future authors the world is waiting for. The rest of us can't go on forever. But unless you take time to learn the techniques of good writing and then sit down and tell the stories inside your head, you may never become a writer. And the rest of us will miss the blessings of what you have to say.

You can do just about anything you set your mind to do. And while writing a book for Adventist young people certainly didn't bring me prosperity, it did bring a feeling of satisfaction that comes from achieving a goal, from doing something I thought only others could do.

Is there something you think is too hard for you? Conquer it! (By persevering.) Think positively. Tell yourself, "I can do it." Imagine yourself having already done it. And before you realize it, you have.

From *Daily Devotional: Out of this World*
by permission of Nancy Beck Irland

Never Give Up

"Oh, brother, what's the use!" cried Tommy angrily as he slammed down his tools, plunged his hands into his trousers pockets and stamped out of his workroom.

"Why, what's the matter?" asked Daddy, guessing by the look on Tommy's face that something had gone wrong.

"Oh, it's that airplane model, Dad," said Tommy. "It just won't go right and I'm through—finished. I won't do another stroke on it."

"That's too bad," said Daddy. "What's gone wrong?"

"Everything's gone wrong," said Tommy viciously. The parts won't fit and the glue won't stick and the paper tears all to pieces. It's just no fun, Dad, that's all. Its one awful mess and I won't touch it again. I'm going to go play ball with the fellows."

"You mean you are going to give up?"

"Yes, I am," said Tommy with decision. "I don't want to make any more airplanes in my life."

"But, Tommy," said Daddy, "that's not the way to talk. You'll never get anywhere that way. Remember the old saying, 'Never give up, never say die.'"

"Dad," said Tommy, "I am all finished with making planes. There's too much fiddle and fuss, and if you don't do everything just right, nothing fits and it's all a mess. So there. I'm going out to play."

"Let me have a look at it," said Daddy. "Maybe it isn't as bad as you think."

"Oh, well, all right," growled Tommy. "You can look at it if you want to, but it's no good, I tell you."

The two went into Tommy's workshop and Daddy began to look over the situation.

"It seems to me," he said after a while, "that you were not careful enough in following the directions. If you had taken more pains to do everything right, you would have saved yourself all this trouble."

At this Daddy took up two pieces of wood that Tommy had torn away as useless and, with a touch here and there with a chisel, he put them together perfectly. "Well, look at that!" exclaimed Tommy. "They fit, don't they?"

"Of course they fit, Tommy," said Daddy. "You just need to take a little more time and a little more care, with a little more determination not to give up."

Daddy went on working with the scattered pieces of wood, cutting here, sandpapering there. Gradually the plane began to take shape—proper shape this time—and Tommy's interest began to revive.

As he worked, Daddy went on talking.

"You known, Tommy," he said, "nobody gets anywhere in this life unless he learns to 'stick it out' even when things seem to go wrong. We all have to hold on until we have conquered our difficulties."

"Um," said Tommy. "The plane's looking better, isn't it, Dad?"

"Yes, it is," said Daddy, quietly going on with his work. "Let me see. Have you heard of the boy who found oil in California?"

"No," said Tommy, his eyes on the plane.

"Well," said Daddy, "I want to tell you about him. This particular boy went out there over seventy years ago. He had a 'hunch' that oil could be found near a place called Ventura. So he and a friend decided to bore a hole in the ground and seek for oil. They had no modern drilling machinery, just an old-fashioned drill and the strength of their arms to drive it into the ground. To draw it out they used the pull of a bent sapling. For thirty days they kept pushing that drill deeper and deeper into the ground, letting the sapling yank it out again each time. It looked hopeless. Many times they must have been tempted to give up. But they didn't, and when they had pushed that drill down thirty feet, they found oil oozing out of the ground."

16

"Mind your fingers with that chisel, Dad," said Tommy. "You'll cut yourself in a minute."

"Thanks; I'm watching," said Daddy, as the plane continued to grow. "And now another thing about those boys in California—When they found they could get only a trickle of oil from the first well, they crossed the valley and started all over again, drilling down thirty feet. Again they got only a trickle of oil. They started drilling once more. This time they got nothing at all—not a drop."

"Pretty hard luck," said Tommy.

"I should say so," said Daddy. "But they didn't give up. They decided that they were not sinking their wells deep enough. They made up their minds that they would keep drilling until they found all the oil they wanted."

"Mind the paper on those wings, Dad; it tears easily."

"I'm minding," said Daddy. "Those two youngsters started drilling yet again. Down and down they went, toiling away day after day, week after week, month after month, with their primitive tools. You'll never guess how deep they went this time."

"A hundred feet?" asked Tommy.

"No. Six hundred feet!" said Daddy. "I don't understand how they did it, but they did. That was sticking it out, if you like."

"Did they strike oil?" asked Tommy.

"They did. It flowed out in torrents, one hundred and fifty barrels a day. It was the beginning of the great oil industry of California. On that day, too, through the determination of those two young fellows, was founded the Standard Oil Company, now known all over the world. Every time we get gas or oil for our car, we should remember we owe it to two boys who wouldn't give up."

"The plane's looking fine, Dad," said Tommy. "I think I could finish it by myself now."

"Good!" said Daddy, passing the work over to Tommy. "That's the spirit. Start again and see it through."

Two days later, when the glue had stuck hard, Tommy was out flying his plane. Somehow there was a special thrill about it. He had won. Of course Daddy had helped a bit, but, after all, he had finished it himself. It wasn't just a mess on the bench, but a real plane. As it soared into the air he whispered something to himself. "Never give up," he said. "Never say die." Tommy never forgot the lesson of the men who tried and tried again until they found oil.

From *Uncle Arthur's Bedtime Stories*
by permission of Review and Herald

More Resources on Perseverance

The resources below may be used during the second week if you would like to include a story on a particular day. You may also choose to use some of these stories if you are only dealing with upper graders during the first week.

The first resource is **Kids of Integrity** http://www.kidsofintegrity.com/perseverance. You will find Bible stories, texts, object lessons, and a variety of other tools which are free. The second source is www.youtube.com I have included two specific stories on perseverance with a few notes. Be sure to review the resources ahead of time. Have Fun!!!

As a faith-filled parent/teacher, you want to help your children develop Christ-like attitudes and behavior. But this important responsibility can seem overwhelming. How do you know where to start?

Kids of Integrity is a set of free resources that will help you coach your kids with confidence and a clear sense of direction. Better still, *Kids of Integrity* will excite your children about living "God's way."

Another resource is www.youtube.com The complete URL for each resource is listed below. If you do not use the resource as listed below you may get something else.

There is no sound to JD's story of perseverance. You can easily use it as a continuing story for two days.

"My athletic story many have found inspirational . . . At the end I share the results from the world master games in Sydney. But I care more about the story than the results since we do not have a choice whether we win or lose, whether we fail or succeed. Only choice we ever have is whether we quit or keep on trying. It was fun . . . jd.causse@yahoo.com for questions." http://www.youtube.com/watch?NR=1&feature=endscreen&v=HFtqN05aUtM

Another example of perseverance is the story of Texas A&M's Calleb Russell. It does have audio and he refers to God several times as he shares his experience of securing a football scholarship. http://www.youtube.com/watch?v=kxtWpvB-0u0

Week Two

Perseverance

```
                           Perseverance

        Introduction    Perseverance        Perseverance
                         Teaching Procedure   Tasks

        Forming Groups   Monday               T-chart

        Roles            Tuesday              Four Corners

        Random Call      Wednesday            Ranking &
        Cards                                 Human Bar
                                              Graph

        Review           Thursday             Either /Or and
                                              Rally Table

                         Friday               Choices, Choices
                                              Choices
```

Forming Groups

During the second week we like to use the process of setting up base or family groups (Johnson, Johnson, & Holubec, 2008), as a part of our class organization. One of the first decisions you will have to make is whether the base groups will be randomly assigned or assigned by set criteria such as similar interests, same grade, different learning styles, or some form of achievement grouping. If you decide on random assignment, there are, of course, many ways to accomplish that task.

Roles

Once the groups are formed, usually in groups of four (that number works best for students in grades 3 and up;), you ask each group to number themselves from 1 to 4, or if there is an odd number, from 1 to 3 or 5. When that has been accomplished, number the roles from 1-4 (we like to assign the roles randomly for the first time), and announce that the members of the group will perform that role. For example, if the social skills monitor was numbered 1, the number 1 person in the group would perform the role of the social skills monitor, the number 2 person would perform the role of recorder, the number 3 person would perform the role of reporter, and the number 4 person would perform the role of materials and environment person. If there are three in a group, one person will have two roles. If there are five in the group, the number 4 person in the group will be in charge of materials and the number 5 person in the group will be in charge of the environment.

Random Call Cards

The cards are collected as soon as they are filled out. Ask the materials person at each table to gather the cards from their group and bring them to you. You announce you will use the cards for two primary purposes; one, for you to get better acquainted with them, and second, as a means to call on them randomly when answers to questions or when reports on assignments need to be presented. As a teacher you need to always have your Random Call cards with you because randomly calling on participants is such an effective process for getting and keeping their attention. For this reason, you want to ensure that all cards are the same in appearance. Avoid using colors or marks that would help participants to discriminate their card from another.

You will want to have a card for each group (table). Each table should have a number and/ or a name. Because each group member now knows the role they perform, you can ask the recorder for the group to write the table number and group name on a 3 x 5 card. It should be, if possible, a different color than the other cards that have their individual names on them. Instruct the recorder to also write the names of their group members on the card. When this is finished, instruct the materials person to bring the card to you. With this card, when it is appropriate to do so, you can call on the groups (tables) in a random manner. Ordinarily, when a table is called on for an answer, the reporter for the group would speak for the group.

Perseverance Teaching Procedure Week 2

Monday

T-Chart

"Now let's use a T-chart to find out what **perseverance** *'looks like'* and *'sounds like.'"* Draw a T-chart, as illustrated on the next page, on chart paper, white board, or on your computer screen. "What will a person say and do when they are showing perseverance? Remember, I am looking for concrete, observable behavior, something that you can hear someone say or see what they do," (See Appendix for a set of step-by-step instructions. Divide groups as needed, i.e., half of the classroom will complete *"looks like"* and the other half *"sounds like"* or 1's and 2's complete *"looks like"* and 3's and 4's will complete *"sounds like."*)

"I will give you 3 minutes to work in your groups. Try to think of 3 or 4 examples. Then I will call on the reporters to give me the responses . . . Time is up. I will use my Random Call cards to decide which table will share first. Then we will continue by using a Round Robin (See Appendix.) allowing each group an opportunity to share one example." (Fill out the T-chart or invite a student who has good writing to fill it in as the teams share their suggestions.)

After completing one round (meaning that each group has had a chance to contribute), you may choose to do another round or you may open the floor for any suggestions which have not yet been recorded. When finished, post the T-chart in the classroom.

"We will post the T-chart where we all can see it. If we think of other examples of what perseverance *'looks like'* or *'sounds like'* during the week, we will add them to the T-chart."

T-Chart

Perseverance

Looks Like	Sounds Like

"Before we have prayer asking God to help us practice **perseverance,** let's review the definition." You may have the entire class repeat it together, boys, then girls, different groups, etc. Remind them to practice perseverance throughout the day and at home. Then finish with prayer.

Tuesday

Four Corners—(often abbreviated as Corners) You will need to write the name of 4 of the stories you read the last week on 81/2 by 11 sheets of paper. You may use white or colored paper.

Never Give Up	Brenda's Skates	Thomas Edison	The Rabbit and the Turtle

"Good morning class!!! It's time for worship. I would like you to use a Think-square-share to discuss how you were **persevering** yesterday or if you noticed anyone else who was **persevering**." (Give them from 30 seconds to 1 1/2 minutes to discuss.) "Now I will use my Random Call cards." (Call on 2-3 students and then open the floor.)

"Today we are going to use a Four Corners activity (See Appendix for step-by-step instructions.) for our worship. You will notice the titles of 4 of the stories we read last week about **perseverance** posted around the classroom, one on each wall. I want you to think of which story was your favorite story about **perseverance**. Be sure to think of as many reasons for your choice as you can. Think individually. That's right; I should not hear any talking. Now that you have had time to think I want you to stand up and walk to the title you chose. Once everyone is standing by the title they chose, I want you to Turn-to-your-neighbor and talk about why you made the choice you did." (You will have to judge how much time they need, but do not give them too much time. Use the raising of your hand or whatever signal you use to get students' attention.)

"Now I will use Random Call cards. If I call your name then your group will begin (or you may begin with the corner that has the most people or least), and then we will continue around the classroom. We will use a Round Robin to call on each corner to give me one reason they heard or they presented . . . You have given some very good reasons. I will open the floor . . . Good work. You may go back to your seats."

Before prayer you may ask the following questions and have the entire class answer, or different groups, or individuals. "What's the word for this week? What is the definition? What is the text in the Bible that tells us we need to be **persevering**? Excellent!! You were able to tell me word for word what the definition of **perseverance** was and the text in the

Bible that tells us we need to **persevere**. Let's bow our heads for prayer as we ask God to help us to continue to be **persevering**."

Wednesday

Ranking—You will need to have a copy of the exercise so each student can access the information and work individually to complete the task of ranking three or more tasks in their order of preference or priority. (See Appendix for step-by-step instructions.)

"This morning we are going to complete a ranking exercise for worship. I would like the materials person to come and take enough of the materials for each person in your group. Each of you needs to answer the question individually. Let's read the question together:

In which of the following places is perseverance most important to you?

_____ Home

_____ School

_____ Church

_____ Sports

"Remember this is about what you think: 1 = most important; 2=next important; 3= next; and 4 is least important. I am going to give you 3 minutes to work individually. After you have completed the task, you may discuss your ranking with your group.

"To complete this exercise let's create a Human Bar Graph. I have four different pieces of paper on a wall/board with each paper having one of the choices written on it. Line up under your number one choice." (Students should be facing you so they form a bar graph. There are many connections you can help the students make at this time. Which has the most people? What can you learn from where people stood?) "Talk-to-your-neighbor and share why you made the choice you did for your number one. I will then call on some of you randomly. You can tell me what you said or what your neighbor said." Even though this is not math class, did you notice how much easier it is to see how the class voted?

"Excellent work!!! You were able to make a choice and explain why that choice was most important to you. You may return to your seat. Let's repeat the word, definition, and text before we have prayer today."

Thursday

Either/Or—You will need to write the words WINTER/ SUMMER on 8 1/2 by 11 sheets of paper. You may use white or colored paper. Post these on opposite sides of the room. (See Appendix for step-by-step instructions.)

WINTER	SUMMER

"For worship today you will be able to participate in an Either/Or exercise. It is one of my favorites. It is like the Four Corners exercise we did on Monday, except that in an Either/Or exercise you only have two choices. Even though you may like both choices, you are forced to choose one and give your reasons for making that choice. Here is the question: For you, is perseverance more like winter or summer?

"Yes, you have to think first and I should hear no talking." (Give them time to think, perhaps 30 seconds.) "Now you may go to the side of your choice. Turn-to-your-neighbor and talk about why you made the choice you did." (You will have to judge how much time they need, but do not give them too much time. Use the raising of your hand or whatever signal you use to get students' attention.)

"We will use a Rally Table (see Appendix for step-by-step instructions) to share your thoughts. In a Rally Table one person from one side gives a reason then another person from the other side shares a reason. Let's begin with those of you who chose summer. Anyone in the group can give a reason they chose summer or a reason someone else in the group chose summer. Good, you were able to give a reason why you chose summer to be more like **perseverance**. Now let's go to the winter side. Give me just one reason. Let's go back to summer. It is like playing tennis, you go back and forth." (Go back and forth (rally) 3 or 4 times, then open the floor. Share your choice at the end too.)

"Well done. You were able to tell why you thought perseverance was more like summer or winter to you. I appreciated hearing all the different ideas. You may go back to your seats." (Before prayer you could find out if they want to add anything else to the T-chart, make comments on those you have seen who have shown **perseverance**, etc.)

Friday

Have each group illustrate **perseverance**. Choices could include:

1. Songs
   a. They can write their own words to a familiar tune or find a song
2. Find or create a story or speech
3. Skits/role play
4. Acronyms
5. Pictorials
6. Power Point presentation or other digital presentations
7. Videos they find or create or,
8. Combinations of these

"Remember, each person in the group has to be involved in the presentation. Have fun and make it memorable."

Special Note: Make this day special. Be creative!!!!!

Week Three & Four

Table of Contents

Week Three

Efficiency

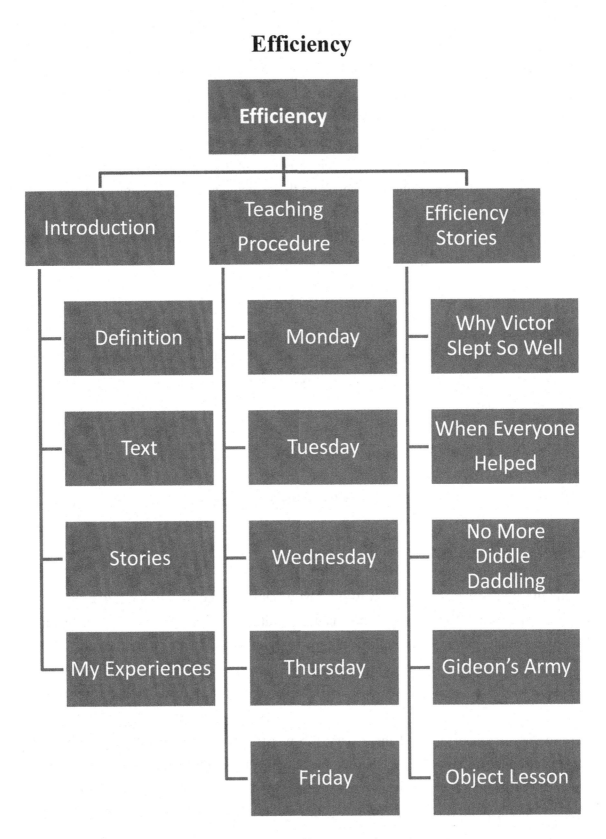

Efficiency

Definition:	The ability to do what needs to be done with a minimum amount of effort or waste; working well.
Attributes:	You: (1) Have a task to complete; (2) Use a minimum amount of effort; (3) Use a minimum amount of time ; and (4) Do it well.
Text:	Ecclesiastes 9:10—"Whatever your hands find to do, do it with your might."*
Stories:	At the end of the week you may ask students to write about their favorite story/object lesson from those that were shared during the week.
My Experiences:	Students write about a personal experience involving the trait for the week. Students may take pictures and post, interview someone and post, prepare a short video, or other media enhanced method to present their experience.

You could also make a digital record of the word, definition, attributes, text, stories, and my experience and post it on the class webpage, wiki, or electronic notebook. However, it is imperative that you create a specific place for worship where students can see the information throughout the day.

* You may use another appropriate text if you choose.

Teaching Procedure Week 3

Monday

"Good morning. Let's review our word for last week by repeating the word, definition, and text from the Bible. Ready, begin. The character trait we studied last week is Perseverance. Perseverance is continuing to do something in spite of obstacles or difficulties and the text in the Bible that helps us to be persevering is Matthew 19:26, 'With God all things are possible.'"

Turn-to-your-neighbor and tell them what the word is for this week. That's correct. The word is **efficiency.** Let's read together the meaning of the word **efficiency** using a complete sentence. **Efficiency** is doing what needs to be done with a minimum amount of effort or waste; working well. Very good. Turn-to-your-neighbor and repeat the meaning of the word

efficiency. Excellent. What does that mean? It means that when you come in the classroom, instead of speaking to your classmates, you put your things away first. It means that if you have many papers to throw away, instead of making three trips to the wastebasket, you take the wastebasket to your desk. It means you sharpen all your pencils before class begins." (Teacher, add anything that you want for your classroom, because that is what they will learn to do.)

"The text in the Bible that encourages us to be *efficient* is Ecclesiastes 9:10—'Whatever your hands find to do, do it with your might.' Let's read it together: Ecclesiastes 9:10 says 'Whatever your hands find to do, do it with your might.' Excellent, you all read the text."

Talk about the weekend or read the story "Why Victor Slept So Well." (p. 38)

Pray—"When we pray, let's ask God to help us be **efficient**."

Tuesday

"I wonder who will be efficient this morning. John is being **efficient**. He is putting his things away quickly. Sally is using bookmarks to mark the pages we will be working on today. Tiffany is already heading her papers for the day. Let's see how **efficient** everyone will be when I say that it is time for worship. 'It's time for worship.' Oh! Look at how quickly this whole group put their things away!"

Use a complete sentence to tell your neighbor the word we are studying this week." (Reply—"The word we are studying this week is **efficiency**.") "Very good. Now use a complete sentence to repeat the definition of **efficiency** to a different neighbor at your table." (I like the way Jake is turning to another neighbor to give the definition.)

"Now everyone has three minutes to learn the word and definition." (Wait three minutes.) "Turn-to-your-neighbor and repeat the definition. Now we will have (choose one person) share with the whole class. Efficiency is the ability to do what needs to be done with a minimum amount of effort or waste; working well." (Make sure everyone has a turn and praise them. Remember to be specific with your praise)

"All of you did such a good job. Let's all say it together." (Reply—"The word we are studying this week is **efficiency**. **Efficiency** is the ability to do what needs to be done with a minimum amount of effort or waste; working well.")

Read "When Everybody Helped" story. (p. 40)

"Next we will use a structure called Think-square-share. I want you to think individually about the answers to the questions about the story." (Give students time to think and then continue.) "You may now square with your group and discuss your responses. The recorder will write and the reporter will report. Social Skills persons, make sure all are involved in squaring."

Ask Questions: Use Think-pair-share. Use Random Call cards to share.

1. Who was efficient in this story? (Literal, Knowledge)
2. How were they efficient in this story? (Comprehension)
3. How can you be efficient in school? (Synthesis, Creative)

Call on different groups (tables, perhaps two) to report—they can each give one example and then open the floor.

"Your assignment is to observe when your classmates or you are practicing **efficiency**. We will talk about it again tomorrow."

Challenge students: "I want you to find some way of being efficient at home this week. Be ready to share it with us on Friday." (TEACHER: Don't be afraid to use personal examples. They need a model. Example—"This morning I was efficient when I . . . or I practiced efficiency when I . . . .")

Pray: Remind students to include the character trait they are working on.

Wednesday

"Good morning, class. This morning, let's say the word and the definition of the word we have been studying without looking at the board. Let's try it. Remember, we must use a complete sentence." (Reply—"The word we are studying this week is **efficiency**, and the definition of the word **efficiency** is the ability to do what needs to be done with a minimum amount of effort or waste, working well.")

"Today, it's going to be harder. I'm going to give you 1 1/2 minutes to learn the verse. Remember you must use a complete sentence. You'll need to say, The text in the Bible that helps us to be **efficient** is Ecclesiastes 9:10—'Whatever your hands find to do, do it with your might.'

"Practice in your head for 11/2 minutes. I will tell you when your time is up. Ready, start. Use a Round Robin to practice the verse.

"Who is ready? I see many hands." (Randomly call on one student. Let everyone try and give them all positive reinforcement. Remember the praise needs to be specific. For example, Ronnie, you were able to say the verse quickly and without any errors. Good work.)

Read: "No More Diddle-Daddling" story (p. 42).

Ask Questions:

Use Think-pair-share. Use Random Call cards to share.

4. Who is efficient in this story? (Literal, Knowledge)
5. In what ways was he/she/ were they efficient? (Comprehension)
6. Have any of you been efficient? In what ways? (Analysis)

Pray: Thank God because students are practicing efficiency, and ask Him to continue to show you how you can be more efficient at school and at home.

Teacher: During the day, always comment on those who are practicing efficiency. For example, Roland is really practicing efficiency. As soon as I said it was time for worship he put his work away and had his eyes on me. Good for you, Roland! Shelley put her things away before going to speak to her friends this morning.

Thursday

"Good morning, class! Let's see who is efficient today. Tim, Ben, Jody, Hannah, etc. are all practicing efficiency. Let's begin with our worship. Today is the day we are trying to say the word, the definition, and the text using a complete sentence and all without looking.

"I'll give you four minutes." (Change the amount of time as needed. If this is your first time, learn it just like the students.) "Let me try, I hope I can do it. **Efficiency** is the ability to do what needs to be done with a minimum amount of effort or waste; working well and the text in the Bible that encourages us to be efficient is Ecclesiastes 9:10—'Whatever your hand finds to do, do it with your might.'

"Who is ready to say it just as I did?" Let everyone try. Those who have difficulty, say, "You are doing it well and just need to study it a little bit more. I'll give you another chance tomorrow. Continue to persevere, you can do it. That's excellent," etc.

Remember when people visit to have students repeat by memory what they are learning. One student can say the word, another the definition, etc. The students enjoy doing it and it is impressive. Remember to take every opportunity to use the word and comment on it.

Read: "Gideon's Army" story. (p. 45)

Use a Think-square-share to answer the following questions:

1. Who was efficient in this story? (Literal, Knowledge)
2. How was the person efficient? (Comprehension)
3. How can practicing efficiency help you be a better student? (Analysis)
4. Who has noticed a classmate who has been efficient? Be sure to include in what ways they were efficient. (Application, Analysis)

"Let's keep working on **perseverance** and **efficiency** all through the day." Give some examples yourself. You need to be sure to include everyone.

Pray: Always include something about efficiency.

Friday

"Good morning, class!" Do something special on this day. Begin with a special activity or invite a visitor to make a special presentation. This may be one way to involve the pastors from the different churches. If you do have the pastor or another visitor come, have the students show what they have learned first.

Repeat the word, definition, and text all together first. Anyone who did not say it the day before let him or her try now. If you have a visitor, have different students recite the different parts. Praise them all for their specific responses.

"Today all of you need to show me where you have written the word, text, definition, stories, and your experience on paper, in your notebook, just as I have it on board. Under stories, write one of the stories you remember that we discussed this week, telling how the person was efficient" (Knowledge, Comprehension). "Under experience, write what you did to be efficient here or at home" (Application). "You may also write the definition and text on another piece of paper and decorate it" (Knowledge, Creativity). "You could give this to one of your parents or another teacher. Who else might enjoy these?" (School staff, lay church members, etc.)

Students may begin writing these as early as Monday but save the decorating of the paper for Friday. You just want them to make a notebook or portfolio. These may be either paper or electronic. Be sure they keep a list of the words so they can review them later.

Special Note: Make this day special. Be creative!!!!!

Stories of Efficiency

Why Victor Slept So Well

In hope of getting work, Victor had gone to a big cattle show, where farmers from miles around came to display their animals, inspect their neighbor's horses and cows, and quietly keep their eyes open for suitable men and boys to help them.

By and by one of the farmers came over to the group of lads among whom Victor was standing, and looked them all over very carefully.

"Want work?" he inquired. "Yes," they chorused.

Then his eye caught sight of Victor, and somehow he was drawn to his open, honest, sunburned face. "How about you, son" Do you know anything about farm work?"

"I can sleep on windy nights," said Victor.

"What do you mean?" asked the farmer shortly. "I can sleep on windy nights," replied Victor calmly.

"The boy's stupid," muttered the farmer, walking away. But Victor's strange words kept ringing in his ears. "I can sleep on windy nights," the farmer muttered to himself. "What on earth does the lad mean?"

A little later he came back to the same group. Victor was still there, good-looking and honest as ever. The farmer decided to try again. Once more he asked Victor to tell him what he knew about farming but again he received the same strange reply: "I can sleep on windy nights."

"Well," said the farmer in exasperation, "you had better come along any way and we'll see what you can do."

So Victor accepted the job and went off to live on the farm. His work was good and the farmer was pleased with him. But one night something happened.

It was late, and everybody had gone to bed to sleep. Presently a gust of wind in the trees awakened the farmer, and instantly, he was on his feet. He sensed immediately that a storm was coming up, and his first thought was for the cattle, his haystacks, and his barns.

Rushing into Victor's bedroom, he found the boy asleep.

"Wake up, wake up!" he cried.

But Victor slept on.

"Wake up, I tell you!" he shouted, becoming angrier every minute. "Can't you hear the wind?"

Still Victor slept.

"I'll fire him in the morning for this, I will," stormed the farmer as he hurried out of the room and down into the farmyard.

But here another surprise awaited him.

No doors were banging in the boisterous wind. All were tightly closed and barred. He opened and peered into the cow barn. In fact, so carefully had someone covered them up that not a wisp of hay had been lost.

Through the darkness and the blinding rain the farmer stamped around his property, expecting every minute to find something wrong, but always finding everything right.

A last, dripping wet, he returned to the house. Going upstairs to Victor's room, he looked in. The boy was still sound asleep.

As the wind continued to howl around the house, the farmer recalled the mysterious words: "I can sleep on windy nights." Suddenly he understood.

The boy had done his work so efficiently that there was nothing for him to worry about. He could sleep in a hurricane or an earthquake. Victor kept his job.

From *Uncle Arthur's Bedtime Stories*
by permission of Review and Herald

When Everybody Helped

"I wished," said dad at breakfast time, "I could get that wood sawed up. It has been lying about for weeks since we cut the tree down, and it makes the yard a dreadful sight."

"Aw," snorted Bert. "I don't want to saw any wood today. I'm so busy. Besides, I promised to go out and play tennis with the Jones boys."

"And I can't saw anything today," said Bill. "You see, I hurt my arm the other day and—."

"But it was your left arm," interposed Dad.

"I know," said Bill, "but, well. I guess my right arm hurts too."

"And I just hate sawing wood, sighed Harry. "I'm too tired anyway. I'm going to play trains today. Sawing wood is the worst job I ever knew."

"And if nobody else is going to saw wood," said Jerry, the youngest, neither am I. I'm going to be busy, too."

"That's just too bad." said Dad. "I had rather hoped to have that wood out of the way today, especially as your vacation will soon be over. But there, have a good time and enjoy yourselves. Mother and I have been planning to go to the seaside this afternoon with all of you if the wood had been finished, but I suppose we can go someday later on."

"Do you think he meant it?" whispered Bert to Bill when they were in the garden after breakfast. "I suppose he did," said Bill. "Why?"

"It would be rather nice to go to the seaside," said Bert. "I can play tennis any day. How about your left arm?"

"Seems to be getting a bit better since breakfast," said Bill.

"That's funny," said Harry. "Somehow I don't feel quite as tired as I thought I did."

"What would you to say to—er—perhaps—cutting up a little of it?"

"I was wondering about that myself," said Bert.

"Let's have a look at the job," said Bill. "Maybe it's not as bad as we thought."

"And I'll help too, if you want me to," piped up Jerry.

So they went over to the fallen tree and looked it over.

"You know," said Bert, if we really set about it, we would have the whole job done in two hours."

"Shall we try it?" asked Bill.

"Let's," they all said together, running off to the tool shed.

A few moments later they were back again with the saw, the ripsaw, the compass saw, and, in fact, every saw they could lay their hands on. Then they divided up the job according to the saws they had found and the size of the branches, and were soon busy as bees.

Dad, chancing to look out of the bathroom window, got the shock of his life. "Mother," he called downstairs, "better start packing that lunch. They'll be done in an hour at this rate." And they were.

From *Uncle Arthur's Bedtime Stories*
by permission of Review and Herald

No More Diddle-Daddling

“ G irls, you must clean your room today.”

“Oh, Mommy. Do we have to?” said Kari.

“It’s too messy. We can’t clean up all this junk,” said Kim.

“Who got it all out?” asked Mommy.

“We did. But it will take us a week to get it put back.”

“Well then, you had better get started,” said Mommy.

Kim and Kari went into their room. “Ugh!” they groaned. “What a mess!” There was a pile of dirty clothes right where Kim and Kari stepped out of their clothes the night before. There were at least ten dolls on top of things, under things and in things.

Socks were scattered on the floor where Kari had dumped them out. She had been trying to find two alike.

Three puzzles had been started but never finished. And then there were pencils and paper, and pens and—

“This is impossible,” said Kim, sitting down on the beanbag chair next to her favorite doll. “My doll needs some clothes on first.” She went over to the doll-clothes drawer and selected a dress, hat, sweater, and booties for her doll.

Kari sat down on the floor and spied the paper basket she had started to make. “It still needs a handle,” she said. “I guess I’ll do that first.”

About an hour later Mommy called, “How’s your room coming, girls?” “Fine,” they said.

Kim put the doll in the baby buggy, and Kari put her finished basket on the shelf. But they still hadn’t touched the dirty clothes, the other nine dolls, the socks, the three half-finished puzzles, and the pencils, and paper, and pens.

"I'm tired of cleaning," said Kim.

"Me too," said Kari. "Let's make a bed in the top of the closet."

"That's a good idea," said Kim.

So they propped the bunk-bed ladder against the wall and climbed up to the top of the closet.

"We can put our dollies to sleep up here," said Kim, smoothing out a blanket. Up and down the ladder they went carrying up blankets and pillows and six dolls. About a half hour later, Mommy called, "How's your room coming, girls?"

"Fine," they said.

But they still hadn't touched the dirty clothes, the other three dolls, the socks, the three half-finished puzzles, and the pencils and paper and pens.

Just then the telephone rang, and the girls could hear Mommy saying, "Oh, how exciting! Yes, I think the children would love to go. Two o'clock? I think we can make it. The girls must finish cleaning their room before we can go. But they have been working on it for over an hour and a half now. It should almost be finished. See you soon. Good-bye."

"Who was that?" the girls called from their perch in the top of the closet.

"That was Aunt Joanie. She and Uncle Dick are going to the mountains for a picnic, and she thought you children might like to go along."

"Yippy, yippy, yippy," the girls shouted. "When can we go?"

"We need to leave in an hour. But your room must be spic and span before that time, or you won't be able to go."

"Oh, what will we do?" cried Kari, looking down on the mess below.

"No more diddle-daddling around," said Kim, let's get this place clean. Mommy means what she says."

And in less than six minutes Kim and Kari had carried down all the blankets and pillows and dolls from the top of the closet.

And in two more minutes the dirty clothes had been picked up and put in the dirty clothes basket in the bathroom.

It took only seven minutes to find all of the ten dolls and line them up neatly on the shelf.

Putting up all those loose socks together was a job. But in ten minutes they were all put away in the sock drawer.

Now the puzzles. Kim and Kari each chose to put one together, it took nine minutes. They decided to cooperate in the last puzzle, and it took only six minutes to finish putting that one together.

Now all that was left were the pencils and paper and pens. They put the pencils in the pencil box and the pens in the pen box and the drawings in one pile and the clean paper in another pile and the mussed up paper in the waste basket.

Then they jumped up and looked around the room and shouted, "We're finished!"

"Good," said Mommy. "You have ten minutes left to change your clothes, comb your hair, get your sweaters and get into the car."

In less than ten minutes they were on their way to the mountains.

"I thought you girls said that it would take a week to clean your room," said Mommy.

Kim and Kari started to giggle as they answered, "That depends on whether you diddle-daddle or not."

(You can say that depends on whether you're EFFICIENT or not.)

From *Kim, Kara, Kevin Storybook*
by permission of Kay Kuzma

Gideon's Army

G ideon was excited; thirty two thousand men had answered the message and joined forces to come and help him deliver the Israelites from the Midianites. Now all the Midianites and the Amalekites and the people of the East had come together to fight Israel.

Gideon knew God was leading him and seeing the thirty-thousand men gave him courage. But then God spoke and said: "You have too many men."

"Too many men!" that didn't seem possible and was hard for Gideon to understand.

"Yes," God told him; "it's too dangerous to fight with so many. When they win they will think it's because of their own strength."

At the Lord's command and to everyone's surprise, Gideon said to the men, "Whosoever is afraid may turn back and leave."

To Gideon's surprise twenty-two thousand men left and only ten thousand remained.

"How can we go against the Midianites with only ten thousand men?" Gideon probably thought.

But God spoke to him again and said: "Gideon, there are still too many men."

How could that be? He had only ten thousand men left.

God said, "Take the men by the stream and those who kneel down to drink water can be sent back home."

Do you know how many men were left after Gideon sent home all the men who stopped to drink the water? There were only 300 men left. And why were they chosen? They were efficient. They did not kneel down to drink but instead stooped down and were ready, and eager to fight.

With God's help Gideon and the three hundred men won a great victory that day.

Are you ready for classes when the bell rings? Are you ready for each class with only the books needed at that time?

Let's ask God to help us to be efficient throughout the day.

Adapted from the Bible (Judges 6)
by Rita Henriquez-Green

More Resources on Efficiency

The resources below may be used during the second week if you would like to include a story on a particular day. You may also choose to use some of these stories/insights if you are only dealing with upper graders during the first week.

Efficiency

Modern life is hectic. We are expected to do so much in so little time. Perhaps that is the reason why we value productivity and efficiency so highly in our society.

The dangers of working mindlessly are greater in our time than before because it is a side effect of the division of labor, a system of working that every modern economy has adopted. Without the ability to understand the overall process of production, workers experience a loss of meaning and do not feel the significance of their work. Boredom and mistakes easily set in. In order for a person to practice creativity and wisdom in their work, it is necessary for the worker to first gain a broad understanding of the complete process.

The second dimension of efficiency is the ability to uncover alternatives. Thinking might seem deceptively like rest, but the mental energy spent thinking will result in efforts saved. A saying by Leonardo Da Vinci illustrates this well, "Men of lofty genius when they are doing the least work are most active." Another famous personality who believes in this is Victor Hugo. He supports this when he says, "A man is not idle because he is absorbed in thought. There is a visible labor and there is an invisible labor."

Since increasing efficiency through creativity can be achieved by looking for alternatives, one good way to gather ideas is through observation. Studying a competitor or a team-mate at work can generate ideas that are both direct and practical. The ability to see other ways of working will enable us to be a better judge of the efficiency of our own methods.

An effective person will not only consider the best method of accomplishing their task at the outset. Such a person will constantly be on the lookout for refinements to the process. Nothing can aid understanding of the job's demands like actually doing it. It is n o surprise that the creative and thinking worker finds involvement in the working process eye-opening.

Last but not least, efficiency is not something detached from daily living to be placed on a lofty pedestal and applauded. Jean Paul Richter exhorts us to "not wait for extraordinary circumstances to do good action; but to try to use ordinary situations." We will soon attain extraordinary efficiency if we possess the dual skill of creative reasoning and the ability to apply it in our daily lives. http://storiesnmore.blogspot.com/2006/07/efficiency.html

Another resource is www.youtube.com The complete URL for each resource is listed below. If you do not use the resource as listed below you may get something else.

Saab Studio Story: Efficiency at Work

One of the great automotive design challenges is reducing drag and improving efficiency while keeping a stylish look. http://www.youtube.com/watch?v=dOI7C7TpUPM

Success Stories—Tony Perrotta

Operational efficiency and a strategic shift have positioned Greentec to prosper in the recovery.

http://www.youtube.com/watch?v=egN1_2wvaXk

Week Four

Efficiency

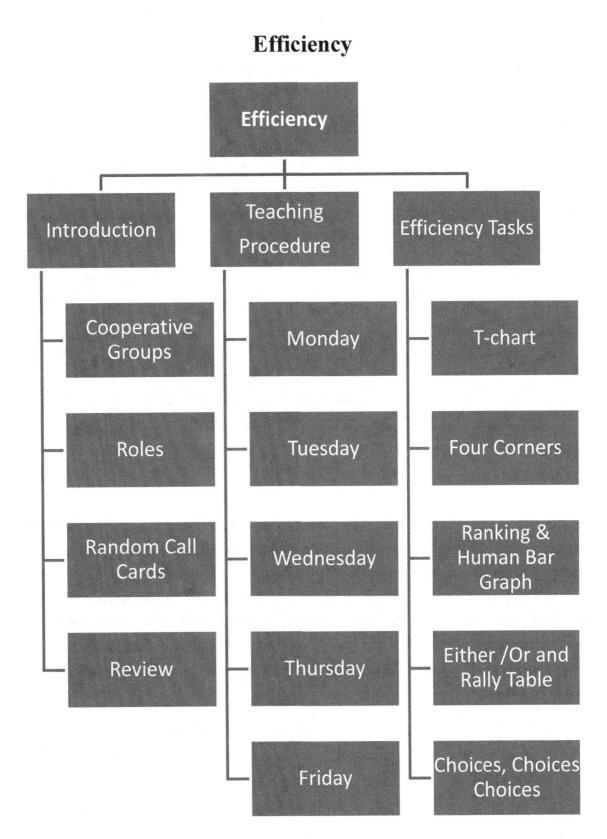

Cooperative Groups

Remember, during the second week we like to use the process of setting up base or family groups (Johnson, Johnson, & Holubec, 2008) as a part of our class organization. If you have not organized the groups yet now would be a good time to do it.

Roles

Now is the time to change roles. The persons in each group still keep the same number however now you change the roles. You continue to rotate through the roles each time you introduce a new character trait (see example below) or you may choose to change roles at the beginning of each week. Post the roles where they can be seen.

Week 1 & 2	Week 3 & 4	Week 5 & 6	Week 7 & 8	Week 9 & 10
Reporter 3	Reporter 2	Reporter 1	Reporter 4	Reporter 3
Recorder 4	Recorder 3	Recorder 2	Recorder 1	Recorder 4
Materials Person 1	Materials Person 4	Materials Person 3	Materials Person 2	Materials Person 1
Social Skills/ Environment 2	Social Skills/ Environment 1	Social Skills/ Environment 4	Social Skills/ Environment 3	Social Skills/ Environment 2

Random Call Cards

Continue to use the Random Call name cards and table cards for two primary purposes; one, for you to get better acquainted with them, and second, as a means to call on them randomly when answers to questions or when reports on assignments need to be presented. As a teacher you need to always have your Random Call cards with you because randomly calling on participants is such an effective process for getting and keeping their attention and ensuring equal participation. For this reason, you want to ensure that all cards are the same in appearance. Avoid using colors or marks that would help participants to discriminate their card from another.

Teaching Procedure Week 4

Monday

T-Chart

"Now let's use a T-chart to find out what **efficiency** '*looks like*' and '*sounds like.*'" (Draw a T-chart as illustrated on the next page on chart paper or on your computer screen.) "What will a person say and do when they are showing **efficiency**? Remember, I am looking for concrete, observable behavior, something that you can hear someone say or see what they do." (Divide groups as needed, i.e., half of the classroom will complete "*looks like*" and the other half "*sounds like*" or 1's and 3's complete "*looks like*" and 2's and 4's will complete "*sounds like,*" etc.)

"I will give you 3 minutes to work in your groups. Try to think of 3 or 4 examples. Then I will call on the reporters to give me the responses . . . Time is up. I will use my Random Call cards to decide which table will share first. Then we will continue by using a Round Robin" (See Appendix.) "Allowing each group an opportunity to share one example." (Fill out the T-chart or invite a student who has good writing to fill it in as the teams share their suggestions.)

After completing one round (meaning that each group has had a chance to contribute), you may choose to do another round or you may open the floor for any suggestions which have not yet been recorded. When finished, post the T-chart in the classroom.

"We will post the T-chart where we all can see it. If we think of other examples of what perseverance '*looks like*' or '*sounds like*' during the week, we will add them to the T-chart."

T-Chart

Efficiency

Looks Like	Sounds Like

"Before we have prayer asking God to help us practice **efficiency**, let's review the definition." You may have the entire class repeat it together, boys, then girls, different groups, etc. Remind them to practice **efficiency** throughout the day and at home. Then finish with prayer.

Tuesday

Four Corners—You will need to write the name of 4 of the stories/activities you read the last week on 8 1/2 by 11 sheets of paper. You may use white or colored paper.

Why Victor Slept So Well	When Everybody Helped	No More Diddle-Daddling	Gideon's Army

"Good morning class!!! It's time for worship. I would like you to use a Think-square-share to discuss how you were **efficient** yesterday or if you noticed anyone else who was **efficient**." (Give them from 30 seconds to 1 1/2 minutes to discuss.) "Now I will use my Random Call cards." (Call on 2-3 students and then open the floor.)

"Today we are going to use a Four Corners activity for our worship. You will notice the titles of 4 of the stories we read last week about **efficiency** posted around the classroom, one on each wall. I want you to think of which story was your favorite story about **efficiency**. Be sure to think of as many reasons for your choice as you can. Think individually. That's right; I should not hear any talking. Now that you have had time to think, I want you to stand up and walk to the title you chose. Once everyone is standing by the title they chose, I want you to Turn-to-your-neighbor and talk about why you made the choice you did." (You will have to judge how much time they need, but do not give them too much time. Use the raising of your hand or whatever signal you use to get students' attention.)

"Now I will use Random Call cards. If I call your name then your group will begin (or you may begin with the corner that has the most people or least), and then we will continue around the classroom. We will use a Round Robin to call on each corner to give me one reason they heard or they presented . . . You have given some very good reasons. I will open the floor . . . You did a good job of giving reasons for your choices. You may go back to your seats."

Before prayer you may ask the following questions and have the entire class answer, or different groups, or individuals. "What's the word for this week? What is the definition? What is the text in the Bible that tells us we need to be efficient? Excellent!!! You were able to tell me word for word what the definition of **efficiency** was and the text in the Bible that tells us we need to **efficient**. Let's bow our heads for prayer as we ask God to help us to continue to be efficient."

Wednesday

Ranking—You will need to have a copy of the exercise so each student can access the information and work individually to complete the task of ranking three or more tasks in their order of preference or priority.

"This morning we are going to complete a ranking exercise for worship. I would like the materials person to come and take enough of the materials for each person in your group. Each of you needs to answer the question individually. Let's read the question together:

Why is it important for you to be efficient in your school work?

_____ So you can get more work done

_____ So you can get good grades

_____ So your teacher/parents will be happy with you

_____ Because it makes you feel good

"To complete this exercise let's create a Human Bar Graph. I have four different pieces of paper on a wall/board with each paper having one of the choices written on it. Line up under your number one choice." (Students should be facing you so they form a bar graph. There are many connections you can help the students make at this time. Which has the most people? What can you learn from where people stood?) "Talk-to-your-neighbor and share why you made the choice you did for your number one. I will then call on some of you randomly. You can tell me what you said or what your neighbor said. Even though this is not math class, did you notice how much easier it is to see how the class voted?" Call on two or three and then open the floor to others who wish to respond.

Pray: Remind students to ask God to help them practice efficiency at home and at school.

Thursday

Either/Or—"You will need to write the words SAVE TIME/ ACCOMPLISH SOMETHING on 8 1/2 by 11 sheets of paper. You may use white or colored paper. Post these on opposite sides of the room.

SAVE TIME	ACCOMPLISH SOMETHING

"For worship today you will be able to participate in an Either/Or exercise. It is one of my favorites. It is like the Four Corners exercise we did on Monday, except that in an Either/Or exercise you only have two choices. Even though you may like both choices, you are forced to choose one and give your reasons for making that choice. Here is the question: What makes you feel happier when you have a difficult task to do and accomplish the task? When you save time so you can do something else or feeling that you accomplished something difficult?

"We will use a Rally Table to share your thoughts. In a Rally Table one person from one side gives a reason then another person from the other side shares a reason. Let's begin with those of you who chose save time. Anyone in the group can give a reason they choose save time or a reason someone else in the group chose save time. Good, you were able to give a reason why you chose save time so you can do something else. Now let's go to accomplish something difficult. Give me just one reason. Let's go back to save time. It is like playing tennis, you go back and forth." (Continue until you stop the process. Share your choice at the end too.)

"Well done. You were able to tell why you feel happier when you save time so you can do something else or why you feel happier when you accomplish something difficult. Being efficient helps us save time and accomplish difficult tasks. You may go back to your seats." (Before prayer you could find out if they want to add anything else to the T-chart, make comments on those you have seen who have continued to build their character, etc.)

Friday

Have each group illustrate **efficiency**. Choices could include creating or finding:

1. Songs
    a. They can write their own words to a familiar tune or find a song
2. Find or create a story or speech
3. Skits/role play
4. Acronyms
5. Pictorials
6. Power Point presentation or other digital presentations
7. Videos they find or create or,
8. Combinations of these

"Remember, each person in the group has to be involved in the presentation. Have fun and make it memorable."

Special Note: Make this day special. Be creative!!!!!

Week Five & Six

Table of Contents

Week Five

Obedience

```
                        ┌──────────────┐
                        │  Obedience   │
                        └──────────────┘
              ┌─────────────────┼─────────────────┐
      ┌──────────────┐  ┌──────────────┐  ┌────────────────────┐
      │ Introduction │  │  Teaching    │  │ Efficiency Stories │
      │              │  │  Procedure   │  │                    │
      └──────────────┘  └──────────────┘  └────────────────────┘
              │                 │                   │
      ┌──────────────┐  ┌──────────────┐  ┌────────────────────┐
      │  Definition  │  │    Monday    │  │  Kevin and the     │
      │              │  │              │  │      Crabs         │
      └──────────────┘  └──────────────┘  └────────────────────┘
              │                 │                   │
      ┌──────────────┐  ┌──────────────┐  ┌────────────────────┐
      │    Text      │  │   Tuesday    │  │   Obedience        │
      │              │  │              │  │   at School        │
      └──────────────┘  └──────────────┘  └────────────────────┘
              │                 │                   │
      ┌──────────────┐  ┌──────────────┐  ┌────────────────────┐
      │   Stories    │  │  Wednesday   │  │ Grandma's Special  │
      │              │  │              │  │     Toy Box        │
      └──────────────┘  └──────────────┘  └────────────────────┘
              │                 │                   │
      ┌──────────────┐  ┌──────────────┐  ┌────────────────────┐
      │My Experiences│  │  Thursday    │  │   Obedience        │
      │              │  │              │  │    at Play         │
      └──────────────┘  └──────────────┘  └────────────────────┘
                                │                   │
                        ┌──────────────┐  ┌────────────────────┐
                        │    Friday    │  │  Object Lesson     │
                        └──────────────┘  └────────────────────┘
```

Obedience

Definition:	Doing willingly what one is told to do.
Attributes:	(1) You are asked to do something; (2) You follow directions; (3) You do it willingly; (4) You do it with a happy spirit; (5) without complaining.
Text:	Hebrews 13:17a—"Obey your leaders and submit to their authority . . ."* NIV
Stories:	At the end of the week you may ask students to write about their favorite story/object lesson from those that were shared during the week.
My Experiences:	Students write about a personal experience involving the trait for the week. Students may take pictures and post, interview someone and post, prepare a short video, or other media enhanced method to present their experience.

You could also make a digital record of the word, definition, attributes, text, stories, and my experience and post it on the class webpage, wiki, or electronic notebook. However, it is imperative that you create a specific place for worship where students can see the information throughout the day.

* You may use another appropriate text if you choose.

Teaching Procedure Week 5

Monday

"Good morning. This is the third character trait we are studying!!! Turn-to-your-neighbor and tell them what the word is for this week. That's correct. The word is **Obedience.** Let's read together the meaning of the word **obedience** using a complete sentence. **Obedience** is doing willingly what one is told to do. There is a word that is very important in this definition. Turn to another neighbor and tell them the word. On the count of three, tell me the word—One, two, three. That's correct. This week we are going to work not only on doing what we are told to do, but we are going to work on doing it willingly. So when I tell you to put your books away, you're going to do it efficiently (quickly) and willingly.

'The text in the Bible that encourages us to be **obedient** is 2 Corinthians 2:9—"Be **obedient** in all things." Let's read it together: 2 Corinthians 2:9 says 'Be obedient in all things.' Excellent, everyone participated in reading the text. Do you realize that if everyone is efficient and obedient, this school would be really clean? Let's work this week on developing obedience."

I want to compliment Jerry on his perseverance in completing all his assignments last week and all of the class for being so efficient this morning. You put all your things away, sharpened your papers, etc. before it was time for worship.

Talk about the weekend or read the story "Kevin and the Crabs." (p. 66)

Pray—"When we pray, let's ask God to help us be efficient."

Tuesday

"Good morning, class! Use a complete sentence to tell your neighbor the word we are studying this week" (Reply—"The word we are studying this week is **obedience**.") "Very good. Now use a complete sentence to repeat the definition of **obedience** to a different neighbor at your table." (I like the way Jake is willingly turning to another neighbor to give the definition.)

"The definition is so short I'm only going to give you two minutes to learn the definition. Now everyone has two minutes to learn the word and definition." (Wait two minutes.) "Turn-to-your-neighbor and repeat the definition. Let's begin with you. **Obedience** is doing willingly what one is told to do." Make sure everyone has a turn and praise them. Remember to be specific with your praise.

"All of you did such a good job. Let's all say it together." (Reply—"The word we are studying this week is **obedience**. **Obedience** is doing willingly what one is told to do.")

"Class, please stand. Wow! Look at how quickly all of you stood up. You may sit down. I'm very proud of you."

Read "**Obedience** at School" story. (p. 68)

Next we will use a structure called Think-square-share. I want you to think individually about the answers to the questions about the story. (See questions below. Give students time to think and then continue.) "You may now square with your group and discuss your responses. The recorder will write and the reporter will report. Social skills persons, make sure all are involved in squaring."

Ask Questions: Use Think-pair-share. Use Random Call cards to share.

1. Who was **obedient** in this story? (Literal, Knowledge)
2. How were they **obedient** in this story? (Comprehension)
3. How can you be **obedient** in school? (Synthesis, Creative)

Call on different groups (tables, perhaps two) to report—they can each give one example and then open the floor.

"Your assignment is to observe when your classmates or you are practicing **obedience**. We will talk about it again tomorrow."

Challenge students: "I want you to find some way of being **obedient** at home this week. Be ready to share it with us on Friday." (TEACHER: Don't be afraid to use personal examples. They need a model. Example—"This morning I was **obedient** when I . . . or I practiced **obedience** when I . . . .")

Pray: Remind students to include the character trait they are working on.

Wednesday

"Good morning, class. This morning, let's say the word and the definition of the word we have been studying without looking at the board. Let's try it. Remember, we must use a complete sentence." (Reply—"The word we are studying this week is **obedience**, and the definition of the word **obedience** is doing willingly what one is told to do.")

"Today, since the verse is short, I'm going to give you one minute to learn the verse. Remember you must use a complete sentence. You'll need to say, the text in the Bible that helps us to be obedient is 2 Corinthians 2:9—'Be obedient in all things.'

"Practice in your head for 1minute. I will tell you when your time is up. Ready, start. Turn-to-your-neighbor and repeat the verse.

"Who is ready? I see many hands." (Randomly call on one student. Let everyone try and give them all positive reinforcement. Remember the praise needs to be specific. For example, Peter, you were able to say the verse quickly and without any errors. Good work.)

Read: "Grandma's Special Toy Box" story (p. 69).

Ask Questions:

Use Think-pair-share. Use Random Call cards to share.

1. Who is **obedient** in this story? (Literal, Knowledge)
2. In what ways was he/she/they **obedient**? (Comprehension)
3. Have any of you been **obedient**? In what ways? (Analysis)

Pray: Always include something about obedience.

Teacher: During the day, always comment on those who are practicing **obedience**. Nancy is practicing **efficiency** and **obedience**. As soon as I said it was time for worship she willingly put her work away and had her eyes on me. Good for you, Nancy! Cherie stopped playing with the ball willingly during the break yesterday.

Thursday

"Good morning, class! I'm so happy to see so many of you practicing efficiency." (This will help those who are not being efficient become efficient.) As soon as I said, "Good Morning," Marty immediately and willingly started putting away what he was doing, and Bevi, who already put her things away, sat very straight. Let's see who is efficient today. Let's begin with our worship. Today is the day we are trying to say the word, the definition, and the text using a complete sentence and all without looking.

"I'll give you two minutes." (Change the amount of time as needed. If this is your first time, take time to learn it just like the students.) "I will be practicing too. Let me try, I hope I can do it. **Obedience** is doing willingly what one is told to do, and the text in the Bible that encourages us to be obedient is 2 Corinthians 2:9—'Be obedient in all things.'"

"Who is ready to say it just as I did?" Let everyone try. Those who have difficulty, say, "You are doing it well and just need to study it a little bit more. I'll give you another chance tomorrow. Continue to persevere, you can do it."

Remember when people visit to have students repeat by memory what they are learning. The students enjoy doing it and it is impressive. Remember to take every opportunity to use the word and comment on it.

Read: "**Obedience** at Play" story. (p. 71)

Use a Think-square-share to answer the following questions:

1. Who was **obedient** in this story? (Literal, Knowledge)
2. How was the person **obedient**? (Comprehension)
3. How can **obedience** help you be a better student? (Analysis)
4. Who has noticed a classmate who has been **obedient**? Be sure to include in what ways he/she was **obedient**. (Evaluation)

"Let's keep working on **perseverance, efficiency,** and **obedience** all through the day." Give some examples yourself. You need to be sure to include everyone.

Pray: Thank God for helping us develop good character traits.

Friday

"Good morning, class!" (Remember, this is a special day!)

How to Make It a Special Day

1. Invite a visitor: pastor, vice-principal, academy teacher, parent, etc.
2. Use the Story Hour CDs and let the students decorate their papers to give away.
3. Let students sit with a friend.
4. Begin with the story "Obedience at Home" before doing anything else.
5. Use some academy students to present a skit.
6. Remember to check the More Resources section for other ideas including lessons and materials.

Repeat the word, definition, and text all together first. Anyone who did not say it the day before let him or her try now. If you have a visitor, have different students recite the different parts. Praise them all for their specific responses.

"Today all of you need to show me where you have written the word, text, definition, stories, and your experience on paper just as I have it on board. Under stories, write one of the stories you remember that we discussed this week, telling how the person was obedient" (Knowledge, Comprehension). "Under experience, write what you did to be obedient here or at home" (Application). "You may also write the definition and text on another piece of paper and decorate it" (Knowledge, Creativity). "You could give this to one of your parents or another teacher. Who else might enjoy these?" (School staff, lay church members, etc.)

Students may begin writing these as early as Monday but save the decorating of the paper for Friday. You just want them to make a notebook or portfolio. These may be either paper and ink or electronic. Be sure they keep a list of the words so they can review them later.

Special Note: Make this day special. Be creative!!!!!

Pray: "Ask God to help us to remember the character traits we've learned."

Stories of Obedience

Kevin and the Crabs

Kevin was playing on the beach with his Daddy and Grandpa. It was a pebble beach and there were many big logs on it, washed up by a recent high tide.

Daddy and Grandpa were trying to move a great big log that must have been thirty feet long and two feet thick. They were digging away the gravel from underneath it so that when the tide would come again, the log would fall into the water and be carried away.

Kevin was working on a log of his own. It was about six feet long and six inches thick. It lay much further down the beach, near the water. Copying Daddy and Grandpa, he dug the gravel from under it and pretty soon a big wave came in and set it afloat. Overjoyed, he gave it a push and off it went into the sea.

He was very proud that he had got his log off the beach while Daddy and Grandpa were still working away at theirs. But the wind and waves soon brought his log back again. So he gave it another push and set it off once more.

Soon he was having a happy time pushing his log off the beach, watching it come back and pushing it off again.

All this time the tide was going out and he followed the water as it went even farther and farther down the beach.

"Careful," cried daddy, "don't go too far!"

"I won't," said Kevin.

"When you see the rocks, come back," said Daddy.

As the tide sank lower the rocks began to appear—just the tops of them at first. Kevin didn't seem to notice them. He was too interested in his log. He kept pushing it off and waiting for it to come back again.

Now the rocks could be clearly seen. Lots of them. Most of them were covered with green slimy seaweed and were very slippery. That didn't trouble Kevin. Somehow he managed to keep his balance on them as he pushed his log out and out again. He had completely forgotten what Daddy had told him—or had he?

Meanwhile, of course, Daddy had been watching him out of the corner of one eye, wondering how far he would go before he finally remembered. Then it happened.

Trying to balance himself on one of those green, slimy rocks, Kevin suddenly slipped and one foot went down on a moving mass of creepy, crawly crabs. He had never seen so many crabs in all his life. They were everywhere, running between the rocks, as far as he could see.

As he tried once more to balance himself on the rocks, he gave a piercing shriek.

"Daddy," he cried. "Come and save me from the crabs!"

Of course Daddy went, moving carefully across the rocks. Then he picked up Kevin and carried him back. Not to the big log where he and Grandpa had been working, but indoors. Right into the bathroom, in fact.

Pretty soon, there were other sounds floating over the beach. So much so that the crabs may well have said to each one another, "Whatever is going on up there?"

Maybe you can guess what it was. Anyway, Kevin hasn't disobeyed Daddy since. At least, not on the beach.

From *Uncle Arthur's Bedtime Stories*
by permission of Review and Herald.

Obedience at School

A voice over the intercom asked Mrs. Harper, Billy's teacher to go to the office. She told the class to remain quiet and finish their work.

"Now is my chance to make the paper airplane that Billy showed me," thought Jeff. As Mrs. Harper left the room, Jeff started to fold a piece of paper into a plane.

Billy looked at his friend Jeff and was surprised. He thought, "Jeff just accepted Christ as his Saviour, at church. He should not be disobeying his teacher."

Jeff had finished folding his paper airplane and was ready to fly it.

"Hey, Jeff," whispered Billy.

"What?" answered Jeff.

"Now that you are a Christian, you ought to know a special Bible verse. It has helped me to do right," explained Billy.

"All right, what is it?" asked Jeff.

Billy recited Proverbs 15:3 "The eyes of the Lord are in every place, beholding the evil and the good." That means God is watching everything we do, wherever we are."

Jeff thought for a moment. Then he put the airplane in his desk and smiled at Billy.

"Thanks for helping me to do what we were told," said Jeff. "You are a real Christian friend."

From A *Child's Book of Character Building—Book 1*
by permission of Association of Christian Schools International.

Grandma's Special Toy Box

Helen was three years old when David was born, she loved her little brother and was always ready to help Mother bathe and dress him. When Mother needed the baby powder or diaper, Helen would say, "I'll get it," and away she would run. Yes, Helen was a good helper with the baby, but there was one thing Helen hadn't learned to do. She hadn't learned to obey Mother all the time.

Mother told Helen to pick up her toys and put them away when she had finished playing with them. I will, Helen always said, but she never obeyed. Mother had to pick them up.

One day Mother said to Helen, "How would you like to go to Grandma's house for a week?"

Helen danced around and around. "A whole week? May I go today?" she asked.

"Yes, Grandma is coming to get you this afternoon," said Mother.

Helen was ready when Grandma came. She always had fun at Grandma's house because Grandma had so many fun things to play with. There was a special toy box with lots of things Helen didn't have at home. After dinner, when it was too late to play outside, Helen could open the toy box.

"Remember, dear," said Grandma, "you must always put the toys away when you finish playing with them."

"Oh, I will," said Helen. She looked inside the box. There was Malinda her favorite doll.

She lifted her gently and gave her a big hug. All evening Helen dressed and undressed Malinda, talking to her just as she talked to Baby David. But at bedtime Malinda was left on the floor.

The next day when Helen looked for Malinda in the toy box, the doll was not there. Grandma simply said, "She wasn't put back in the box last night."

"Oh, well, I can play with the modeling clay," said Helen. All evening she made funny little clay people and animals. But at bedtime the clay figures were left on the table.

Every day that week, toys disappeared. By Thursday there was nothing left to play with in the toy box. Malinda, the clay, the puzzles, the jack-in-the-box, the games, and the crayons and coloring books were gone. The box was empty. Big tears rolled down Helen's cheeks. "I don't have anything to play with tonight," she cried.

"I'm sorry dear," said Grandma. "You promised to put the toys away and I asked you to, but you didn't obey. Children must learn to obey their parents and (teachers) and grandparents so they will learn to obey God too."

Helen threw her arms around Grandma's neck. "I'm sorry. I'll put them away next time," she said. "May I play with Malinda now?"

"Not tonight," said Grandma. "I want you to think about obeying for a little while. Maybe by tomorrow night you will remember."

Friday night Helen held Malinda tightly. "I'm going to put you away tonight," she whispered. "And I'll try to remember to obey because it makes me happy when I do."

From *Living and Learning*
by Sadie Engen by permission of Review and Herald.

Obedience at Play

"Oh no, it's stuck!" exclaimed Billy.

Billy had just hit a softball so high that it almost went over the roof of the shed. It had hit the peak of the roof and rolled down into the gutter.

Billy loves to play softball. He can play it anytime of the day and all day, if his mother lets him. One thing she will not let him do is let him climb up the shed roof. It is dangerous, she says, and his father has told him that he must call for help if a ball ever gets caught up there.

"Now, what are we going to do?" a friend complained.

"Well, we will have to do what my father told me to do," answered Billy. "Go for help."

Off he ran to his father. The other boys shook their heads. They didn't understand why he couldn't just sneak up on the roof. Who would find out?

Billy came back with his father and a ladder. In a jiffy, the ball was retrieved.

Billy's father was so glad that his son had obeyed his words. As a reward, he decided to join the boys in their game of softball. Now, even Billy's friends are glad he obeyed.

> From *A Child's Book of Character Building—Book 1*
> by permission of Association of Christian Schools International.

Obedience at Home

"Hey, Mike," shouted Billy. "Look what I found!"

Mike glanced up from playing in his yard, to see his friend Billy climbing out on a limb of the old maple tree.

"It looks like a robin's nest. Do you want me to show you the eggs?" said Billy.

"Didn't your father tell you not to climb that tree?" Mike responded.

"Well, yes," answered Billy. "I'll be careful. I'll put the eggs back before he gets home. Besides, you took four robin's eggs to school last week."

"I know I did, but didn't you hear what happened?" Mike replied.

"No what happened?" asked Billy, as he stopped climbing just before reaching the nest.

"I was so proud of my robin's eggs that I showed them to everyone," explained Mike. "One of the eggs dropped when I was showing it to my friends. Two more were broken when I fell while riding my bike."

Mike continued, "Later, when my father found out, he had me place the remaining eggs back in the nest and watch it. The mother robin wouldn't go near it. Father told me that birds will never return to their eggs when they have been touched by people."

"So that's why my father told me to stay away from our robin's nest!" Billy thought aloud.

"I had better climb down," Billy concluded. "There are many reasons why it is wise to obey Father's rules."

[From *A Child's Book of Character Building—Book 1*
by permission of Association of Christian Schools International]

More Resources on Obedience

The resources below may be used during the second week if you would like to include a story on a particular day. You may also choose to use some of these stories if you are only dealing with upper graders during the first week.

The first resource is **Kids of Integrity** http://www.kidsofintegrity.com/obedience. You will find Bible stories, texts, object lessons, and a variety of other tools which are free. The second source is www.youtube.com. I have included two specific stories on obedience with a few notes. Be sure to review the resources ahead of time. Have Fun!!!

As a faith-filled parent/teacher, you want to help your children develop Christ-like attitudes and behavior. But this important responsibility can seem overwhelming. How do you know where to start?

Kids of Integrity is a set of free resources that will help you coach your kids with confidence and a clear sense of direction. Better still, *Kids of Integrity* will excite your children about living "God's way."

Another resource is www.youtube.com The complete URL for each resource is listed below. If you do not use the resource as listed below you may get something else.

In the story below Elijah Kaneshiro, a four year old boy, tells a story about obeying his parents. We can all learn from his conclusions.
http://www.youtube.com/watch?v=Im4MKCo2aNk

Another example you can use with older students is titled "The Gallon of Milk." It is the story of a man who got to experience God's miracle by a simple prayer and obeying God despite the doubts. Students have to read the story from the screen. http://www.youtube.com/watch?v=KpuytosRESI

Obedience

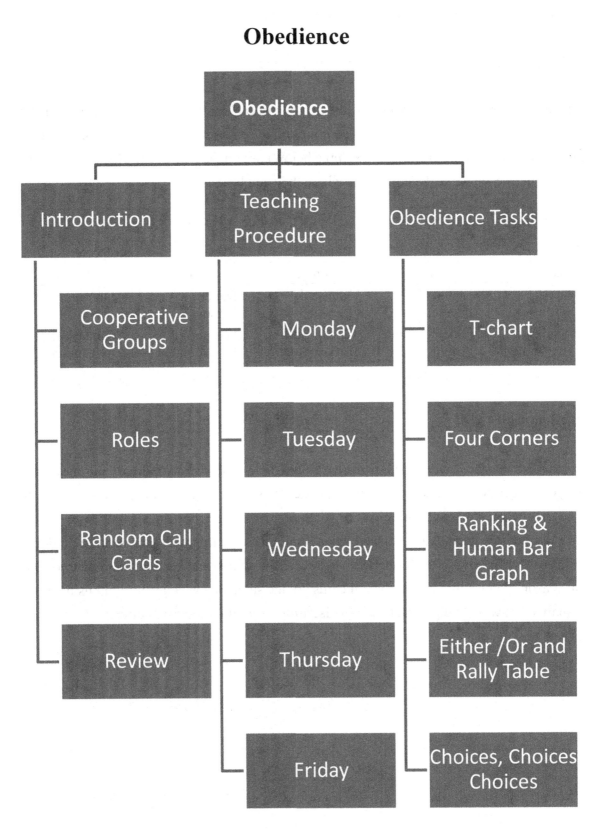

Cooperative Groups

Continue to reinforce the use of cooperative groups.

Roles

It is time to change roles. Remember, the persons in each group still keep the same number however now you change the roles. You continue to rotate through the roles each time you introduce a new character trait (see example below) or you may choose to change roles at the beginning of each week. Post the roles where they can be seen.

Week 1 & 2	Week 3 & 4	Week 5 & 6	Week 7 & 8	Week 9 & 10
Reporter 3	Reporter 2	Reporter 1	Reporter 4	Reporter 3
Recorder 4	Recorder 3	Recorder 2	Recorder 1	Recorder 4
Materials Person 1	Materials Person 4	Materials Person 3	Materials Person 2	Materials Person 1
Social Skills/ Environment 2	Social Skills/ Environment 1	Social Skills/ Environment 4	Social Skills/ Environment 3	Social Skills/ Environment 2

Random Call Cards

Continue to use the Random Call name cards and table cards for two primary purposes; one, for you to get better acquainted with the students, and second, as a means to call on them randomly when answers to questions or when reports on assignments need to be presented. As a teacher you need to always have your Random Call cards with you because randomly calling on participants is such an effective process for getting and keeping their attention. For this reason, you want to ensure that all cards are the same in appearance. Avoid using colors or marks that would help participants to discriminate their card from another.

Teaching Procedure Week Six

Monday

T-Chart

"Now let's use a T-chart to find out what **obedience** '*looks like*' and '*sounds like.*'" (Draw a T-chart as illustrated on the next page on chart paper or on your computer screen.) "What will a person say and do when they are **obedient**? Remember, I am looking for concrete, observable behavior, something that you can hear someone say or see what they do." (Divide groups as needed, i.e., half of the classroom will complete "*looks like*" and the other half "*sounds like*" or 1's and 3's complete "*looks like*" and 2's and 4's will complete "*sounds like,*" etc.)

"I will give you 3 minutes to work in your groups. Try to think of 3 or 4 examples. Then I will call on the reporters to give me the responses . . . Time is up. I will use my Random Call cards to decide which table will share first. Then we will continue by using a Round Robin" (See Appendix.) "Allowing each group an opportunity to share one example." (Fill out the T-chart or invite a student who has good writing to fill it in as the teams share their suggestions.)

After completing one round (meaning that each group has had a chance to contribute), you may choose to do another round or you may open the floor for any suggestions which have not yet been recorded. When finished, post the T-chart in the classroom.

We will post the T-chart where we all can see it. If we think of other examples of what perseverance "*looks like*" or "*sounds like*" during the week, we will add them to the T-chart.

T-Chart

Obedience

Looks Like	Sounds Like

"Before we have prayer asking God to help us practice **obedience**, let's review the definition." You may have the entire class repeat it together, boys, then girls, different groups, etc. Remind them to practice **obedience** throughout the day and at home. Then finish with prayer.

Tuesday

Four Corners—You will need to write the name of 4 of the stories you read last week on 8 1/2 by 11 sheets of paper. You may use white or colored paper.

Kevin and the Crabs	Obedience at School/Play	Grandma's Special Toy Box	Obedience at Home

"Good morning class!!! It's time for worship. I would like you to use a Think-square-share to discuss how you were **obedient** yesterday or if you noticed anyone else who was **obedient.**" (Give them from 30 seconds to 1 1/2 minutes to discuss.) "Now I will use my Random Call cards." (Call on 2-3 students and then open the floor.)

"Today we are going to use a Four Corners activity for our worship. You will notice the titles of 4 of the stories we read last week about **obedience** posted around the classroom, one on each wall. I want you to think of which story was your favorite story about **obedience**. Be sure to think of as many reasons for your choice as you can. Think individually. That's right; I should not hear any talking . . . Now that you have had time to think I want you to stand up and walk to the title you chose. Once everyone is standing by the title they chose, I want you to Turn-to-your-neighbor and talk about why you made the choice you did." (You will have to judge how much time they need, but do not give them too much time. Use the raising of your hand or whatever signal you use to get students' attention.)

"Now I will use Random Call cards. If I call your name then your group will begin (or you may begin with the corner that has the most people or least), and then we will continue around the classroom. We will use a Round Robin to call on each corner to give me one reason they heard or they presented . . . You have given some very good reasons. I will open the floor . . . Good work. You may go back to your seats."

Before prayer you may ask the following questions and have the entire class answer, or different groups, or individuals. "What's the word for this week? What is the definition? What is the text in the Bible that tells us we need to be **obedient**? Excellent!!! You were able to tell me word for word the definition of **obedience** and the text in the Bible that tells us we need to be **obedient**. Let's bow our heads for prayer as we ask God to help us to continue to be **obedient**."

Wednesday

Ranking—You will need to have a copy of the exercise so each student can access the information and work individually to complete the task of ranking three or more tasks in their order of preference or priority.

"This morning we are going to complete a ranking exercise for worship. I would like the materials person to come and take enough of the materials for each person in your group. Each of you needs to answer the question individually. Let's read the question together:

Doing willingly what you are told to do in school will:

_____ Keep you safe

_____ Help you not to get into trouble

_____ Help you get your work done easier

_____ Make others like you

"To complete this exercise let's create a Human Bar Graph. I have four different pieces of paper on a wall/board with each paper having one of the choices written on it. Line up under your number one choice." (Students should be facing you so they form a bar graph. There are many connections you can help the students make at this time. Which has the most people? What can you learn from where people stood?)

"Talk-to-your-neighbor and share why you made the choice you did for your number one. I will then call on some of you randomly. You can tell me what you said or what your neighbor said. Even though this is not math class, did you notice how much easier it is to see how the class voted?" Call on two or three and then open the floor to others who wish to respond.

Pray: Remember to ask God to help us to obey willingly.

Thursday

Either/Or—You will need to write the words FRIENDS/ALONE on 8 1/2 by 11 sheets of paper. You may use white or colored paper. Post these on opposite sides of the room.

FRIENDS	ALONE

"For worship today you will be able to participate in an Either/Or exercise. It is one of my favorites. It is like the Four Corners exercise we did on Monday, except that in an Either/Or exercise you only have two choices. Even though you may like both choices, you are forced to choose one and give your reasons for making that choice. Here is the question: is it easier for you to obey when you are with friends or alone?

"We will use a Rally Table to share your thoughts. In a Rally Table one person from one side gives a reason then another person from the other side shares a reason. Let's begin with those of you who chose friends. Anyone in the group can give a reason they choose friends or a reason someone else in the group chose friends. Good, you were able to give a reason why it is easier to obey when you are with friends. Now let's go to alone. Give me just one reason. Let's go back to friends. It is like playing tennis, you go back and forth." (Continue until you stop the process. Share your choice at the end too.)

"Well done. You were able to tell why it is easier for you to do willingly what you are told to do when you are with friends or alone. You may go back to your seats." (Before prayer you could find out if they want to add anything else to the T-chart, make comments on those you have seen who have continued to build their character, etc.)

Friday

Have each group illustrate **obedience**. Choices could include creating or finding:

1. Songs
    a. They can write their own words to a familiar tune or find a song
2. Find or create a story or speech
3. Skits/role play
4. Acronyms
5. Pictorials
6. Power Point presentation or other digital presentations
7. Videos they find or create or,
8. Combinations of these

"Remember, each person in the group has to be involved in the presentation. Have fun and make it memorable."

Special Note: Make this day special. Be creative!!!!!

Week Seven & Eight

Table of Contents

Week Seven

Attentiveness

Attentiveness

- Introduction
  - Definition
  - Text
  - Stories
  - My Experiences
- Teaching Procedure
  - Monday
  - Tuesday
  - Wednesday
  - Thursday
  - Friday
- Attentiveness Stories
  - Attentiveness at Play
  - The Man Who Listened
  - Attentiveness at School
  - Attentiveness at Home
  - Object Lesson

Attentiveness

Definition:	Listening with the ears, eyes, and heart.
Attributes:	(1) You are not talking; (2) You look at the person who is talking; (3) You focus on what the person is saying.
Text:	James 1:19—". . . Everyone should be quick to listen, slow to speak and slow to become angry." You may also use Proverbs 1:5—"Let the wise listen and add to their learning."* NIV
Stories:	At the end of the week you may ask students to write about their favorite story/object lesson from those that were shared during the week.
My Experiences:	Students write about a personal experience involving the character trait for the week. Students may take pictures and post, interview someone and post, prepare a short video, or other media enhanced method to present their experience.

You could also make a digital record of the word, definition, attributes, text, stories, and my experience and post it on the class webpage, wiki, or electronic notebook. However, it is imperative that you create a specific place for worship where students can see the information throughout the day.

* You may use another appropriate text if you choose.

Teaching Procedure Week 7

Monday

"Good morning. Let's review our word for last week by repeating the word, definition, and text from the Bible. Ready, begin. The character trait we studied last week was Obedience. Obedience is doing willingly what one is told to do and the text in the Bible that helps us to be obedient is 2 Corinthians 2:9 "Be obedient in all things."

This week we're going to be working on one of my favorite words. It's also one of the hardest for students and grown-ups too. Turn-to-your-neighbor and tell them what the word is for this week. That's correct. The word is **attentiveness.** I think the definition will tell us why it is so hard to do. Let's read together the meaning of the word **attentiveness** using a complete sentence. **Attentiveness** is listening with the ears, eyes, and heart. I like that definition. Let's say it again. Attentiveness is listening with the ears, eyes, and heart. Have you ever said to your older brother or Dad, 'I have something to tell you,' you start speaking and he keeps reading the newspaper or watching T.V.? How does it make you feel? You want his full attention.

"It is one of the most important traits for us to learn. The Bible commands us to listen. Let's read our text for this week. James 1:19 says, 'Everyone should be quick to listen, slow to speak and slow to become angry.'

"What is another word for **attentiveness**?" (Reply—"listening") "If I say I want everyone's attention, I want you to be what?" (Reply—"**attentive**"). "I'm going to say that during the day and we'll see if you can already start working on attentiveness."

Read: "Attentiveness at Play" story or talk about weekend happenings. (p. 93)

Pray: "Let's ask God to help us learn to be attentive."

Tuesday

"It's time for worship. Oh! Look at how quickly this whole group put their things away! You were being **attentive**, **obedient**, and **efficient**.

"Use a complete sentence to tell your neighbor the word we are studying this week" (Reply—"The word we are studying this week is **attentiveness**.") "Very good. Now use a complete sentence to repeat the definition of **attentiveness** to a different neighbor at your table." (I like the way Lonna is turning to another neighbor to give the definition.)

"Now everyone has two minutes to learn the word and definition." (Wait two minutes.) "Turn-to-your-neighbor and repeat the definition. Let's begin with you. **Attentiveness** is listening with your ears, eyes, and heart." Make sure everyone has a turn and praise them. Remember to be specific with your praise.

"All of you did such a good job. Let's all say it together." (Reply—"The word we are studying this week is **attentiveness**. **Attentiveness** is listening with your ears, eyes, and heart.")

Read "The Man Who Listened" story. (p. 94)

"Next we will use a structure called Think-square-share. I want you to think individually about examples of **attentiveness** in the story." (Give students 30 seconds to think and then continue.) "You may now square with your group and discuss your responses. The recorder will write and the reporter will report. The social skills persons will make sure each person in the group gives at least one idea."

Call on different groups (tables, perhaps two) to report—they can each give one example and then open the floor.

Think-pair-square-share—"How can you be **attentive** right here in the classroom?" Use Random Call cards to share responses.

"Your assignment is to observe when your classmates or you are practicing **attentiveness**. We will talk about it again tomorrow."

Challenge students: "I want you to practice **attentiveness** at home this week. Be ready to share it with us on Friday." (TEACHER: Don't be afraid to use personal examples. They need a model. Example—"This morning I was **attentive** when one of the teachers came to me with a question, I stopped what I was doing, I looked at her and focused on what she was saying.")

Pray: Let's ask God to help us be attentive.

Wednesday

"Good morning, class. I'd like everyone's **attention**. Excellent, this group of students has all their eyes on me. That is a good sign that you are listening with your ears, eyes, and heart.

"Let's all say the text together for this week. Remember you must use a complete sentence. You'll need to say, The text in the Bible that helps us to be **attentive** is James 1:19— . . . 'Everyone should be quick to listen, slow to speak and slow to become angry.' Practice in your head for 2 minutes. I will tell you when your time is up. Ready, start." Use a Round Robin to practice the verse.

"Who is ready? I see many hands." (Randomly call on one student. Let everyone try and give them all positive reinforcement. Remember the praise needs to be specific. For example, Benjamin, you were able to say the verse quickly and without any errors. Good work.)

Read: "**Attentiveness a**t School" story (p. 95).

Ask Questions:

Use Think-pair-share. Use Random Call cards to share.

1. Who is **attentive** in this story? (Literal, Knowledge)
2. In what ways was he/she/ were they **attentive**? (Comprehension)
3. Have any of you been **attentive** this week? In what ways? (Application, Analysis)

Pray: Let's ask God to help us be attentive at school.

Teacher: During the day, always comment on those who are practicing any of the traits. "Hannah is really practicing attentiveness. As soon as I said it was time for worship she put her work away and had her eyes on me. Good for you, Hannah! (Comment either on a few more students, group, or class.)

Thursday

"Good morning, class! Let's see who is attentive today. Lonna, Jerry, Jake, etc. are all practicing attentiveness. Let's begin with our worship. Today is the day we are trying to say the word, the definition, and the text using a complete sentence and all without looking at the board.

"I'll give you four minutes." (Change the amount of time as needed.) "Remember, everyone must use a complete sentence. Let's say it together. Our word for this week is **attentiveness**. **Attentiveness** is listening with the ears, eyes, and heart. The text in the Bible that tells us to be **attentive** is James 1:19— . . . 'Everyone should be quick to listen, slow to speak and slow to become angry.' Practice individually for two minutes and then practice with your group.

"Who is ready to say it just like we practiced?" Let everyone try. Those who have difficulty, say, "You are doing it well and just need to study it a little bit more. I'll give you another chance tomorrow. Continue to persevere, you can do it. That's excellent," etc.)

Remember to take every opportunity to use the word and comment on it.

Read: "**Attentiveness** at Home" story. (p. 96)

Use a Think-square-share and Random Call cards to answer the following questions:

1. Who was **attentive** in this story? (Knowledge/Literal)
2. How was the person **attentive**? (Comprehension)
3. How can **attentiveness** help you at home? (Analysis)
4. Who has noticed a classmate who has been **attentive**? Be sure to include in what ways they were **attentive**. (Evaluation, Critical)

"Let's keep working on **perseverance, efficiency, obedience,** and **attentiveness** all through the day. Give some examples yourself. You need to be sure to include everyone."

Pray: Thank God for helping us know about the importance of being attentive.

Friday

"Good morning, class!" (Remember, this is a special day!)

How to Make It a Special Day

1. Invite a visitor: pastor, vice-principal, academy teacher, parent, etc.
2. Use the Story Hour CD's and let the students decorate their papers to give away.
3. Let students sit with a friend.
4. Begin with the story "Attentiveness in the Bible" before doing anything else.
5. Use some academy students to present a skit.
6. Remember to check the More Resources section for other ideas including lessons and materials.

NEW IDEA
Conduct a Quiz Bowl

Equipment Needed:

1. Bowl to put questions in
2. Timer—person who keeps time (a watch, clock or one of several free computer versions)
3. Scorekeeper—person who keeps the score
4. Two teams—players needed for game
5. Judge (optional) decides if answers are acceptable.

Each team is allowed 15 seconds to answer. If you give team A a question, and they miss the answer, team B may answer. If they get it wrong, the teacher gives the answer before going to the next question. If team B gets it right, they still get the next question. Whichever team accumulates 10 points first is declared the winner. Answers must be very specific. The first answer given out loud is the one taken, or you may prefer to have each team appoint a spokesperson.

Suggested Questions for Quiz Bowl

1. Recite Matthew 19:26.
2. Name a story that shows perseverance in the Bible.
3. Give the definition for efficiency.
4. Name the 3rd word we studied.
5. What are all these words that we are studying called?
6. Which character trait is one of the teacher's favorites?
7. Which text encourages us to practice attentiveness?
8. What is a synonym for attentiveness?
9. Who can define perseverance?
10. Recite Ecclesiastes 9:10

Stories of Attentiveness

Attentiveness at Play

One day, Tina's family visited a park so that they could go hiking. At the entrance, a ranger gave careful instructions. He said children should always stay with their patents. The woods were thick. It was easy to get lost or hurt. But Tina did not listen attentively as the ranger was talking.

Soon, the Baker family started on their hike through the woods. It was great fun. Tina was last in line as they walked up and down the paths. She would stop, look, and linger. It wasn't long until her family was far ahead of her, out of sight.

She came upon a beautiful stream near the path. Tina decided to go across. She noticed some rocks in the water. They looked just big enough to step on. Slowly, she jumped from one to another. She was in the middle of the stream when she heard a noise. It was a large, strange dog. He began to bark and growl at her. Tina became so afraid that she almost slipped off the rock. Just then, a boy came running up. He chased the dog away and helped Tina get back to the bank.

Then Tina's father came running to find her. He was glad no one was hurt. He scolded Tina for not being attentive to the ranger's instructions.

Tina's family continued their hike; but, this time, Tina was the first in line.

From *A Child's Book of Character Building—Book 1*
by permission of Association of Christian Schools International

The Man Who Listened

Naaman's wife was crying and looked so sad that one of the slave girls asked her what was wrong.

"Oh", she replied, "my husband has a horrible disease and no one can cure him. He has leprosy and he is going to die. There is nothing we can do!"

"I know someone who can help him."

Naaman's wife just shook her head in despair, but the slave girl continued to talk. "The prophet Elisha can heal your husband. You see, he is a prophet of the true God of heaven. The true God is a wonderful God. If we listen and follow his directions, all things are possible. Not long ago Elisha even raised a dead boy to life."

Her mistress was so touched that she told the story to one of the servants who told her husband. Although Naaman didn't think it was possible, everyone encouraged him to go to Elisha.

Finally Naaman found himself at Elisha's door. Elisha sent a message telling him that if he washed in the river Jordan seven times he would be cured.

"I can't believe this man just sent me, the captain of the army of Syria, a message. He should have come and personally talked with me. Instead he tells me to wash in a river in Israel, but our rivers are much better."

Although Naaman was upset the servants convinced him to listen to the prophet and to obey him. So Naaman turned his chariot around and went to the river Jordan. He dipped in the water once, twice, (count with me) three times, four times, five times, six times, seven times and Wow, the seventh time, the leprosy was gone!

Naaman was so filled with gratitude, he admitted, "Now I know that there is no God in all the earth, but in Israel." Naaman was very thankful that he listened to the man of God.

Based on 2 Kings, Chapter 5, from *A Child's Book of Character Building—Book 1* *by* permission of Association of Christian Schools International

Attentiveness at School

Art class is Tina's favorite. The teacher, Mr. Cook, always has new and fun things to do. His students are allowed to talk quietly while working. There is one time when Mr. Cook does not want any talking: that is when he is giving directions. He wants everyone to be attentive.

One Monday, Mr. Cook was explaining how to mix paint. Tina was trying hard to be attentive, but Alex was not. He was looking out the window. Finally, Mr. Cook finished, and the class began painting.

Tina painted a picnic scene. She mixed bright sunny colors, just as Mr. Cook had shown her.

Alex was having trouble with his painting. He didn't know how to mix dark colors for the storm he was painting.

Tina came over to Alex's desk and asked if she could help. He said, no, it was too late. His picture was ruined.

"You could have made your stormy picture look darker by adding black to all your colors," advised Tina. "Mr. Cook showed us how. Next time, you'll have to be more attentive to the teacher."

Now Alex was sorry he had not listened or watched his teacher. He told Tina that the next time he would be attentive, and his storm picture would be terrific.

From *A Child's Book of Character Building—Book 1*
by permission of Association of Christian Schools International

Attentiveness at Home

"Tina, come here," called Mrs. Baker. "Oh, no! I really want to play with my doll and bottle. I'll pretend I didn't hear," thought Tina.

"Tina, come here, now!" called Mother a second time.

But Tina was not listening and continued to play. Just then, Mrs. Baker walked into the room, with a sad look on her face.

"Tina," said Mother, "why didn't you come when I called you?"

"Tina, it is always important to come when I call," said Mother. "You must learn to listen attentively and obey."

Tina saw that her mother was sad and disappointed. "I called you, and you chose not to obey my call," said Mother. "Jesus is very sad. He wants you to listen and obey, too."

Now Tina felt sad. "I am sorry, Mother," she said. "Will you pray with me as I ask Jesus to forgive me?" They prayed, and then she asked her mother to forgive her, too.

Later, Mrs. Baker called Tina. This time, Tina listened and responded to her mother's call. As she ran into the kitchen to find out what Mother wanted, Mother hugged her for being prompt and attentive.

From *A Child's Book of Character Building—Book 1*
by permission of Association of Christian Schools International

Attentiveness in the Bible

"Jesus, Son of Nazareth, Thou Son of David, have mercy on me," cried blind Bartimeeus. (See Mark 10: 46-52)

"Oh, be quiet, Bartimaeus. Stop calling. You're just a blind beggar," scolded people in the crowds. Bartimaeus would not be quiet.

Jesus of Nazareth was passing nearby. He made the lame walk, healed lepers, returned the dead to life. Bartimaeus, too, wanted to be healed.

Loudly he cried out, "Thou Son of David, have mercy on me."

Through the noise of the crowd, Jesus heard and paid attention to the cries of the beggar. He stood still and commanded him to be brought to Him.

"Good news, Bartimaeus. Jesus wants to see you," said a man in the crowd.

The blind man quickly stood up and was led to Jesus. Jesus looked at him and asked, "What do you want me to do for you?"

"Lord, give me my sight," Bartimaeus replied. Lovingly, Jesus answered him, "Your faith has made you well."

Immediately, he could see! Bartimaeus followed Jesus, praising God for what He had done.

From *A Child's Book of Character Building—Book 1*
by permission of Association of Christian Schools International

More Resources on Attentiveness

The resources below may be used during the second week if you would like to include a story on a particular day. You may also choose to use some of these stories if you are only dealing with upper graders during the first week.

The first resource is **Kids of Integrity** http://www.kidsofintegrity.com/attentiveness. You will find Bible stories, texts, object lessons, and a variety of other tools which are free. The second source is www.youtube.com I have included two specific stories and one video clip on attentiveness with a few notes. Be sure to review the resources ahead of time. Have Fun!!!

As a faith-filled parent/teacher, you want to help your children develop Christ-like attitudes and behavior. But this important responsibility can seem overwhelming. How do you know where to start?

Kids of Integrity is a set of free resources that will help you coach your kids with confidence and a clear sense of direction. Better still, *Kids of Integrity* will excite your children about living "God's way."

Internet Resource—A story for older kids

"The Redneck Hunters—A Story About the Importance of Listening" http://betterlifecoachingblog.com/2011/07/29/the-redneck-hunters-a-story-about-the-importance-of-listening/

July 29, 2011 in Great Stories | Tags: listening

John C. Maxwell tells this story in his book, *Leadership Gold.*

A couple of redneck hunters are out in the woods when one of them falls to the ground.

He doesn't seem to be breathing and his eyes are rolled back in his head.

The other redneck starts to panic, then whips out his cell phone and calls 911.

He frantically blurts out to the operator, "My friend Bubba is dead! What can I do?"

The operator, trying to calm him down says, "Take it easy. I can help. Just listen to me and follow my instructions. First, let's make sure he's dead."

There's a short pause, and then the operator hears a loud gunshot!

The redneck comes back on the line and says, "OK, now what?"

Sometimes, it's easy to hear the words without listening to the real message.

We think that we know what's being said, but we don't clarify the situation before jumping to unnecessary and unhelpful conclusions.

We were given two ears and one mouth for a reason. Let's become better and more skilled listeners.

In doing so, we'll improve our relationships, have a better understanding of each other and reduce confusion.

For further reading, here are 5 Tips for Becoming a More Effective Listener http://betterlifecoachingblog.com/2010/07/14/5-tips-for-becoming-a-more-effective-listener/.

For all ages:

An amusing clip which shows a young girl trying to get her grandfather's attention during a performance http://www.youtube.com/watch?v=OQ8ALjl_Xbg (length = 1 minute 20 seconds).

Week Eight

Attentiveness

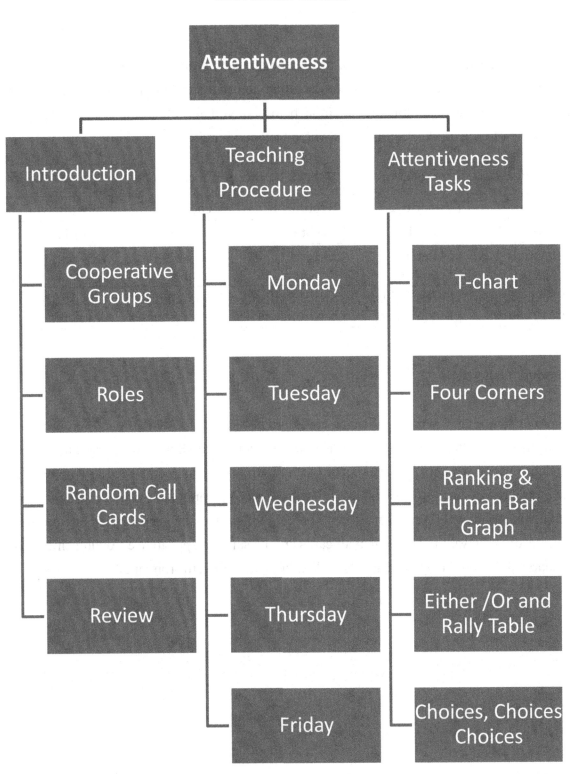

Cooperative Groups

Continue to reinforce the use of cooperative groups.

Roles

It is time to change roles. Remember, the persons in each group still keep the same number however now you change the roles. You continue to rotate through the roles each time you introduce a new character trait (see example below) or you may choose to change roles at the beginning of each week. Post the roles where they can be seen.

Week 1 & 2	Week 3 & 4	Week 5 & 6	Week 7 & 8	Week 9 & 10
Reporter 3	Reporter 2	Reporter 1	Reporter 4	Reporter 3
Recorder 4	Recorder 3	Recorder 2	Recorder 1	Recorder 4
Materials Person 1	Materials Person 4	Materials Person 3	Materials Person 2	Materials Person 1
Social Skills/ Environment 2	Social Skills/ Environment 1	Social Skills/ Environment 4	Social Skills/ Environment 3	Social Skills/ Environment 2

Random Call Cards

Continue to use the Random Call name cards and table cards for two primary purposes; one, for you to get better acquainted with the students, and second, as a means to call on them randomly when answers to questions or when reports on assignments need to be presented. As a teacher you need to always have your Random Call cards with you because randomly calling on participants is such an effective process for getting and keeping their attention. For this reason, you want to ensure that all cards are the same in appearance. Avoid using colors or marks that would help participants to discriminate their card from another.

Teaching Procedure Week Eight

Monday

T-Chart

"Now let's use a T-chart to find out what **attentiveness** '*looks like*' and '*sounds like.*'" (Draw a T-chart as illustrated on the next page on chart paper or on your computer screen.) "What will a person say and do when they are showing **attentiveness**? Remember, I am looking for concrete, observable behavior, something that you can hear someone say or see what they do." (Divide groups as needed, i.e., half of the classroom will complete *"looks like"* and the other half *"sounds like"* or 1's and 3's complete *"looks like"* 2's and 4's will complete *"sounds like"* etc.)

"I will give you 3 minutes to work in your groups. Try to think of 3 or 4 examples. Then I will call on the reporters to give me the responses . . . Time is up. I will use my Random Call cards to decide which table will share first. Then we will continue by using a Round Robin" (See Appendix.) "Allowing each group an opportunity to share one example." (Fill out the T-chart or invite a student who has good writing to fill it in as the teams share their suggestions.)

After completing one round (meaning that each group has had a chance to contribute), you may choose to do another round or you may open the floor for any suggestions which have not yet been recorded. When finished, post the T-chart in the classroom.

"We will post the T-chart where we all can see it. If we think of other examples of what attentiveness '*looks like*' or '*sounds like*' during the week, we will add them to the T-chart."

T-Chart	
Attentiveness	
Looks Like	**Sounds Like**

"Before we have prayer asking God to help us practice **attentiveness**, let's review the definition." You may have the entire class repeat it together, boys, then girls, different groups, etc. Remind them to practice **attentiveness** throughout the day and at home. Then finish with prayer.

Tuesday

Four Corners—You will need to write the name of 4 of the stories read last week on 81/2 by 11 sheets of paper. You may use white or colored paper.

Attentiveness at Play	The Man Who Listened	Attentiveness at School	Attentiveness at Home

"Good morning class!!! It's time for worship. I would like you to use a Think-square-share to discuss how you were **attentive** yesterday or if you noticed anyone else who was **attentive**." (Give them from 30 seconds to 11/2 minutes to discuss.) "Now I will use my Random Call cards." (Call on 2-3 students and then open the floor.)

"Today we are going to use a Four Corners activity for our worship. You will notice the titles of 4 of the stories we used for worship last week posted around the classroom, one on each wall. I want you to think of which story is your favorite. Be sure to think of as many reasons for your choice as you can. Think individually. That's right; I should not hear any talking. Now that you have had time to think I want you to stand up and walk to the story you chose. Once everyone is standing by the story they chose, I want you to Turn-to-your-neighbor and talk about why you made the choice you did." (You will have to judge how much time they need, but do not give them too much time. Use the raising of your hand or whatever signal you use to get students' attention.)

"Now I will use Random Call cards. If I call your name then your group will begin (or you may begin with the corner that has the most people or least), and then we will continue around the classroom. We will use a Round Robin to call on each corner to give me one reason they heard or they presented . . . You have given some very good reasons. I will open the floor . . . Good work. You may go back to your seats."

Before prayer you may ask the following questions and have the entire class answer, or different groups, or individuals. "What's the word for this week? What is the definition? What is the text in the Bible that tells us we need to be attentive? Excellent!!! You were able to tell me word for word the definition for **attentiveness** and the text in the Bible that tells us we need to be **attentive**. Let's bow our heads for prayer as we ask God to help us to continue to **attentive**."

Wednesday

Ranking—You will need to have a copy of the exercise so each student can access the information and work individually to complete the task of ranking three or more tasks in their order of preference or priority.

"This morning we are going to complete a ranking exercise for worship. I would like the materials person to come and take enough of the materials for each person in your group. Each of you needs to answer the question individually. Let's read the question together:

Which is most important to you when learning to be attentive? Listening with your:

_____ Ears

_____ Eyes

_____ Heart

"Remember this is about what you think: 1 = most important; 2 = next important; 3 = next; I am going to give you 3 minutes to work individually. After you have completed the task, you may discuss your ranking with your group . . .

"To complete this exercise let's create a Human Bar Graph. I have three different pieces of paper on a wall/board with each paper having one of the choices written on it. Line up under your number one choice." (Students should be facing you so they form a bar graph. There are many connections you can help the students make at this time. Which has the most people? What can you learn from where people stood?) "Talk-to-your-neighbor and share why you made the choice you did for your number one. I will then call on some of you randomly. You can tell me what you said or what your neighbor said. Even though this is not math class, did you notice how much easier it is to see how the class voted?" Call on two or three and then open the floor to others who wish to respond.

"Excellent work!!! You were able to make a choice and explain why that choice was most important to you. You may return to your seat. Let's repeat the word, definition, and text before we have prayer today." Make any other observations that are appropriate to the lesson.

Thursday

Either/Or—You will need to write the words EASY/ HARD on 8 1/2 by 11 sheets of paper. You may use white or colored paper. Post these on opposite sides of the room.

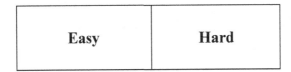

Easy	Hard

"For worship today you will be able to participate in an Either/Or exercise. It is one of my favorites. It is like the Four Corners exercise we did on Monday, except that in an Either/Or exercise you only have two choices. Even though you may like both choices, you are forced to choose one and give your reasons for making that choice. Here is the question: For you, is attentiveness easy or hard to practice?"

"Yes, you have to think first and I should hear no talking." (Give them time to think, perhaps 30 seconds.) "Now you may go to the side of your choice. Turn-to-your-neighbor and talk about why you made the choice you did." You will have to judge how much time they need, but do not give them too much time. Use the raising of your hand or whatever signal you use to get students' attention.

"We will use a Rally Table to share your thoughts. In a Rally Table one person from one side gives a reason then another person from the other side shares a reason. Let's begin with those of you who chose easy. Anyone in the group can give a reason they chose easy or a reason someone else in the group chose easy. Good, you were able to give a reason why attentiveness is easy for you to practice. Now let's go to those who chose hard. Give me just one reason. Let's go back to the other side. It is like playing tennis, you go back and forth." Call on two or three and then open the floor to others who wish to respond. Share your choice at the end too.

"Well done. You were able to tell why you thought attentiveness is easy or hard to practice. I appreciated hearing all the different ideas. You may go back to your seats." (Before prayer you could find out if they want to add anything else to the T-chart, make comments on those you have seen who have shown attentiveness, etc.)

Friday

Have each group illustrate **Attentiveness**. Choices could include creating or finding:

1. Songs
   a. They can write their own words to a familiar tune or find a song
2. Find or create a story or speech
3. Skits/role play
4. Acronyms
5. Pictorials
6. Power Point presentation or other digital presentations
7. Videos they find or create or,
8. Combinations of these

"Remember, each person in the group has to be involved in the presentation. Have fun and make it memorable."

Special Note: Make this day special. Be creative!!!!!

Week Nine & Ten

Table of Contents

Week Nine

Week Ten

Week Nine

Character

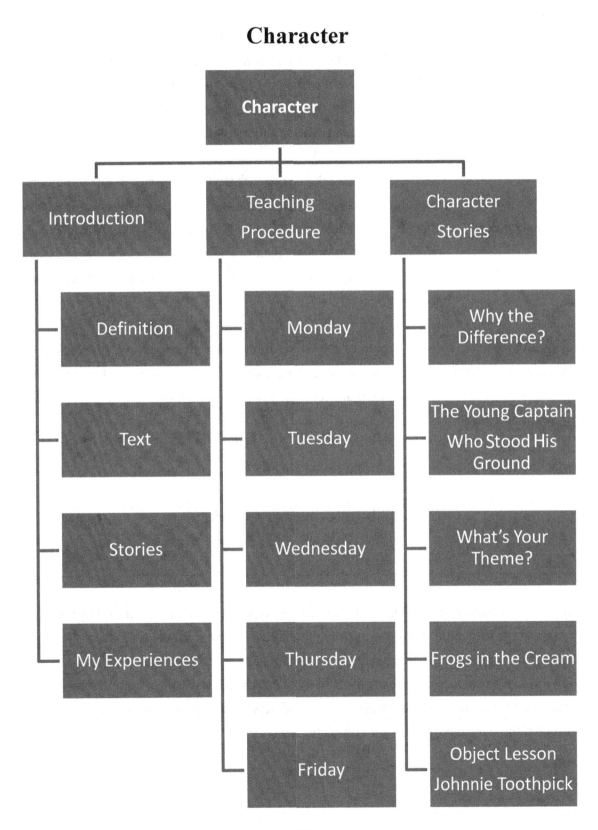

Character

Definition:	The way a person feels, thinks, and acts.
Attributes:	What people think about you (reputation) based upon; (1) Your attitude; (2) What you think; and (3) How you act (behavior).
Text:	Philippians 4:8—"Fix your thoughts on what is true and good and right. Think about things that are pure and lovely, and dwell on the fine, good things in others. Think about all you can praise God for and be glad about."* TLB
Stories:	At the end of the week you may ask students to write about their favorite story/object lesson from those that were shared during the week.
My Experiences:	Students write about a personal experience involving the trait for the week. Students may take pictures and post, interview someone and post, prepare a short video, or other media enhanced method to present their experience.

You could also make a digital record of the word, definition, attributes, text, stories, and my experience and post it on the class webpage, wiki, or electronic notebook. However, it is imperative that you create a specific place for worship where students can see the information throughout the day.

* You may use another appropriate text if you choose.

Teaching Procedure Week 9

Monday

"This week we will be studying a very special word. It isn't a character trait, but it is what character traits help build. Turn-to-your-neighbor and tell them what the word is for this week. That's correct. The word is **character**. Let's all repeat it together using a complete sentence. Good job. Let's read together the meaning of the word **character** using a complete sentence." (**Character** is the way a person feels, thinks, and acts.) "Very good. Turn-to-your-neighbor and repeat the meaning of the word **character**. Excellent.

"Now let's read the text in the Bible that tells us how we should feel, think, and act. The text in the Bible that tells us how we should feel, think and act is Philippians 4:8—'Fix your thoughts on what is true and good and right. Think about things that are pure, lovely, and dwell on the fine, good things in others. Think about all you can praise God for and be glad about.'

"Now, turn to a different neighbor at your table and tell them the text in the Bible that that tells us how we should feel, think and act." (Remember, use a complete sentence.) "The text in the Bible that tells us how we should feel, think, and act is Philippians 4:8—'Fix your thoughts on what is true and good and right. Think about things that are pure, lovely, and dwell on the fine, good things in others. Think about all you can praise God for and be glad about.'"

Talk about the weekend or read "Why the Difference?" story. (p. 117)

Pray—When we pray, let's ask God to help us develop good character.

Tuesday

"Good morning, class! Let's see who is practicing efficiency. Very good." (You may use specific names or group I see that the 2nd row or groups 3 and 4 have put their things away and are sitting straight, etc . . .) I want to tell you how proud I am because so many of you have really been working on developing the character traits we are studying.

"Now use a complete sentence to tell your neighbor the word we are studying this week." (Reply—"The word we are studying this week is **character.**") "Very good. Now use a complete sentence to repeat the definition of **character** to a different neighbor at your table." (The word we are studying this week is **character** and **character** is the way a person feels, think, and acts.)

"This morning I'm going to give the class three minutes to memorize the word and definition. Work individually for 2 minutes and then work with a partner for 1 minute. I will give you the signal. Ready, go." After two minutes give them the signal to let them know they may work with a partner.

"Who is ready?" (Give everyone a chance.) "All of you did such a good job. Let's all say it together." (Reply—"The word we are studying this week is **character. Character** is the way a person feels, think, and acts.")

Read: "The Young Captain Who Stood His Ground. (p. 120)

"Next we will use a structure called Think-square-share. I want you to think individually about the answers to the questions about the story." (Give students time to think and then continue.) "You may now square with your group and discuss your responses. The recorder will write and reporter will report. Social skills persons, make sure all are involved in squaring."

Ask Questions: Use Think-square-share. Use Random Call cards or call on the reporters.

1. What **character** trait is demonstrated in this story? (Literal, Knowledge)
2. How did the trait help in this story? (Comprehension)
3. How can this trait help you? (Analysis, Interpretive)
4. What can you do at home or at school to help develop **character**? (Synthesis, Creative).

Pray: Let's ask God to help us develop **character** in our lives.

Wednesday

"Good morning. Turn-to-your-neighbor and tell them the trait we talked about yesterday? Good job, I could hear everyone talking to a neighbor. This week we will be studying and hearing about many different traits, because all of them help build character. Today is the day we memorize and recite our text. I will give you a little more time today because the text is longer and it is so important. If you can learn to do what this text says, you and all those around you will be very happy people.

"Let's use a complete sentence and read the text together. The text in the Bible that tells us to develop good character is Philippians 4:8—'Fix your thoughts on what is true and good and right. Think about things that are pure and lovely, and dwell on the fine, good things in others. Think about all you can praise God for and be happy about.' I will give you five minutes to learn the text." (Give everyone a chance to say the text and really praise them.)

Read: "What's Your Theme?" story. (p. 122)

Ask Questions: Use Think-square-share. Use Random Call ards or call on the reporters.

1. What **character** trait is demonstrated in this story? (Literal, Knowledge)
2. How did the trait help in this story? (Comprehension)
3. How can this trait help you? (Analysis, Interpretive)
4. What can you do at home or at school to help develop **character**?(Synthesis, Creative).

Pray: Thank God for the example he has given us to follow so we will know how to develop our **character**.

Thursday
_____

"Good morning, class! I am so proud of this group because . . . ." (Be specific.) "Today is one of the most challenging days for you. You are trying to say the word, the definition, and the text using a complete sentence by memory. You should know it all, so it is a matter of practicing it. I will practice too.

"I'll give you five minutes." (Change the amount of time as needed.) "Remember, everyone must use a complete sentence. Let's say it together. Our word for this week is **character**. **Character** is the way a person feels, thinks, and acts and the text in the Bible that tells us how to develop proper **character** is Philippians 4:8—'Fix your thoughts on what is true and good and right. Think about things that are pure and lovely, and dwell on the fine, good things in others. Think about all you can praise God for and be glad about.' Practice individually for two minutes and then practice with your group.

"Who is ready to say it just like we practiced?" Let everyone try. Those who have difficulty, say, "You are doing it well and just need to study it a little bit more. I'll give you another chance tomorrow. Continue to persevere, you can do it. That's excellent," etc.

Remember to take every opportunity to use the word and comment on it.

Read: "Frog in the Cream" story. (p. 123)

115

Use a Think-square-share and Random Call cards to answer the following questions:

1. What character trait is illustrated in this story? (Knowledge/Literal)
2. Why is it important to develop this trait? (Critical, Evaluation)
3. How did it help in the story? (Analysis)

Pray: Let's ask God to help us develop character.

Teacher: For Friday you need to collect and/or prepare the materials you may need.

Friday

"Good morning, class!" (Remember, this is a special day!)

How to Make It a Special Day

OPTION 1:

Read "Johnny Toothpick," using all the suggested props. (p. 124)

OPTION 2:

1. Put a marble in an empty catsup bottle. Turn the bottle upside-down and it will come out. Make the marble move around the sides of the bottle. If it moves fast enough, it stays in, even when the bottle is upside down. If the bottle is idle, it falls out.
2. Show a flash light with bad batteries and good ones. People may look the same on the outside, but whether they shine in the world or not depends on what is inside.

Stories of Character

Why the Difference?

_____

Peter, Paul and Philip were all about the same size and the same age, they all lived within a stone's throw of one another.

They had grown up together, playing the same games and going to the same school. Now, being big and husky, they all decided to do something to help their country; so they went down to the docks and asked for work.

The manager liked the looks of the boys and hired them, offering them the same rate of pay.

Several weeks went by. Then one day the three fathers of the boys began to compare notes.

"How much is your boy earning?" said Peter's father.

"Twenty dollars a week," said Paul's father. "That isn't so bad for a beginner, and they have given him a five-dollar raise already. What's Peter getting?"

"Only fifteen," said Peter's father in disgust. "I'd like to know why. Doesn't seem fair to me. I wonder what they're paying Philip."

"I hardly like to say," said Philip's father. "But Philip tells me that they have just raised his rate to twenty-five dollars a week."

"Twenty-five!" exclaimed Peter's father, getting quite red in the face. "Just think of that! And Peter is getting only fifteen! I'll go down first thing tomorrow morning and tell the manager what I think of him."

So Peter's father phoned the manager and made an appointment to meet him at ten o'clock the next morning. Every moment till then he became more and more angry as he thought of all the terrible things he would say to the manager when he should meet him.

But the manager guessed why he had come. "I suppose you want to know why your boy is being paid only fifteen dollars a week while the other two boys from your district have been advanced," he said.

"Yes, indeed," said Peter's father, "and I think it's . . ."

"Never mind saying what you think," said the manager. "How long can you spend here?"

"Just as long as I have in order to see that justice is done," said Peter's father.

"Well, it may take an hour or two," said the manager. "Just take a seat in this side room and keep out of sight, and watch what happens."

Taken by surprise, Peter's father did not know what else to do but obey. He sat down where he could watch all that went on in the office without being observed.

Meanwhile the manager had pressed a button under his desk. Soon the door opened and in walked Peter. His father watched as the boy slouched up to the desk.

"There's a ship just coming in the harbor, due to dock shortly," said the manager. "Get me full particulars and report in half an hour."

"All right," said Peter, and shuffled out.

As minutes slipped by, Peter's father wondered just what sort of report his boy would bring back. Imagine his surprise when, the half hour up, there was no sign of Peter. The boy seemed to have forgotten all about his instructions.

The manager pressed the button again and told a secretary to send for Paul. The boy arrived and stood attentively in front of the manager's desk.

"There's a ship just coming in the harbor, due to dock shortly," repeated the manager. "Get me full particulars and report in half an hour."

Again the minutes slipped by. As the time limit was almost up, Paul returned.

"The ship has just docked, sir," he said. "She's a big ship and quite heavily loaded with cargo."

"Is that all?"

"That's all."

"Thank you. You may go."

Then the manager pressed his bell the third time, and after a brief pause in came Philip.

"Good morning, Sir," said the boy with a smile. "What can I do for you, Sir?"

The manager repeated his request for full particulars about the incoming ship and asked Philip to be back as soon as possible with complete information.

Twenty minutes later Philip was back in the manager's office again.

"Well, Philip," said the manager, "what did you find out about that ship?"

"She's a 10,000-ton freighter, sir. Last port of call was Cape Town, South Africa. She docked at 10:10 a.m. Cargo is chiefly oranges and other fruit. There are a hundred men busy unloading her now, sir. The Captain wants to sail again one week from tonight. Repairs are needed to the radio and the boiler room."

"Thank you, Philip that is what I wanted to know. You are excused."

"And now," said the manager, turning to Peter's father, "do you require any further explanation of the difference in wage rates?"

"No, I don't," said Peter's father. "But I would like to know where Peter is and why he did not come back."

"So would I," said the manager. "Perhaps you can find out why he loafs on his job."

"I think you can leave that to me," said Peter's father, with a purposeful tone in his voice. "I'll look after him."

And he did.

From *Uncle Arthur's Bedtime Stories*
by permission of Review and Herald

The Young Captain Who Stood His Ground

Back in the early 1800's the people who lived in New Salem, Illinois, found themselves and others who lived on the other frontier at war with the Indians. The Indians, led by Chief Black Hawk, had burned down many of the settler's cabins and left many bloody scalps. So a volunteer company of soldiers, a small group from the hundred or so inhabitants of New Salem, organized to go fight the Indians.

The small group of soldiers needed a leader, so they elected a young man to be their captain. Then they set off to do battle. After a few days of trampling through the wilderness, they spotted an Indian heading toward their camp. Some of the soldiers started to fire but were ordered by their captains not to do so.

When the Indian arrived in the camp, it turned out that he had a pass to allow him safe conduct through the lines. He was a courier. Upon learning that the Indian had safe passage assured through their lines, many of the men in the group of soldiers became very angry and wanted o kill the Indian anyway. "Our orders were to kill the Indians. Here's an Indian. Let's kill him. The only good Indian is a dead Indian."

The group moved forward and began to seize the Indian. Their captain stepped between the group of soldiers and the Indian. "Let the Indian alone," he said. The young captain knew that the position he was taking was a dangerous one. He remembered that he was not an official appointed officer, but one elected by the group that wanted to take the life of an Indian.

There were a few moments of silence. How would the soldiers react to their captain's orders? Would they ignore them, or obey them? Would the captain loose his position, possibly even his life in defending the Indian? Slowly, one by one, the soldiers began to back off. They watched as the young, tall, lanky, captain stood his ground. Each one knew that to get the Indian would mean a battle with the young captain. Several of the soldiers in the group were stronger physically than the young captain. But none of them decided to carry through with the desire to kill the Indian because the captain stood his ground.

The Indian owed his life to the man of character who defended him. Left to himself, he was hopeless. But because there was one person who knew the right and chose to do the right, his life was spared.

One wonders how many times character has been victor over brute strength. Certainly, more times than not. Character, the becoming of a person of moral excellence, is certainly a goal to be pursued.

Even the poorest person with the poorest health can be a person of high character.

Character, of course, cannot be bought. It can only be earned. The soldiers in that small company had learned to respect their captain. They knew that he always stood for that which he believed to be right. He was a man of character. The captains name? Abraham Lincoln.

Taken from *Words of Gold*
by Donald E. Wildmon

What's Your Theme?

Since Christians are humans, we come in a variety of colors, shapes and sizes. A lot of Christians are like wheelbarrows—not good unless pushed.

Some are like canoes—they need to be paddled.
Some are like kites—if you don't keep a string on them, they fly away.

Some are like kittens—they are more contented when petted.
Some are like football—you can't tell which direction they'll bounce next.

Some are like balloons—full of wind and ready to blow up.
Some are like trailers—they have to be pulled.

Some are like the lights—they keep going on and off.
And there are those who always let the Holy Spirit lead them.

Which kind of Christian are you? Which kind do you think Jesus was?
Whether or not we are aware of it, each of our lives has a pattern to it—a theme that we sometimes follow subconsciously. Some people carry a grudge and are always suspicious of others. Some of us live to serve. And some people just live, with no goals, no plans,—they just let life happen.

If we listen to the things we say, we can come up with a pretty clear picture of the theme of our lives—whether we think positively or negatively, and whether or not we are an uplifting influence or a depressing one.

Not surprisingly, the first and last recorded words of Jesus show that His life was focused on one thing: doing the will of God. What are the first recorded words of Jesus? "I must be about my father's business."

And what are his last words? "It is finished."

To do God's will should be the focus of our lives, too. What have you done, or what will you do today, that nobody but a Christian could do?

From Daily Devotional *Out of this World*
by permission of Nancy Beck Irland

Frogs in the Cream

" Perhaps you've heard the story of the two frogs that fell into a butter churn filled with cream. "It's cold!" one of the frogs squeaked to the other. "It's deep and cold! And the sides are so slippery and steep; we'll never get out alive!"

"Keep on paddling. We'll get out of this mess some way," the other frog croaked. "Maybe someone will see us." And around and around he swam.

"It's no use!" the other frog squeaked. Too thin to jump. Too slippery to crawl. We're bound to die sometime anyway, so it may as well be tonight." He sunk to the bottom of the churn and died.

The other frog blinked slowly, clearing the cream from his eyes. Keeping his nose above the cream, he paddled steadily. "I'll swim a while," he said to himself. "It really wouldn't help the world if one more frog was dead."

He paddled all night long with his eyes closed. By morning he was perched on a mass of butter that he had churned all by himself. There he was with a grin on his face, eating the flies that came swarming from every direction.

The little frog had discovered what many of us ignore: if you stick to the task long enough, you're going to be a winner.

Those who keep on believing in God will be winners too. Keep on paddling, never losing faith in God's promises.

From Daily Devotional *Out of this World*
by permission of Nancy Beck Irland

Johnnie Toothpick—Object Lesson

" Thou hast been faithful over a few things. I will make thee ruler over many things."
Matthew 25:23 KJV

Materials needed:

Empty grapefruit half
½ pound gumdrops
1 box of toothpicks
1 toothpick holder
1 attractive dish; 1 small dish
1 thin slice raw potato or soap, cut 1 inch square
Pickle or olives

How to Prepare:

Place the grapefruit half on the attractive dish, rind side up. Stick toothpicks through gumdrops, if small about two gumdrops to a pick, choosing different colors. Stick the toothpicks into the grapefruit rind until it is well covered with the bright colors.

Cut the pickle in small pieces and stick a toothpick in each place; place in small dish.

Wrap some of the cotton around the ends of the other picks and place in holder.

Stick one plain toothpick (no candy) in the slice of potato. This is Johnny Toothpick.

All objects should be kept in a small box.

All people who are Christians should be willing to be of service to others, in little things as well as big things.

Let us learn a lesson from a very special friend. (Lift Johnnie Toothpick—pick a slice of potato—out of the box.) This is Johnnie Toothpick. He is a very humble servant to all, and is found in just about every home. Toothpicks cost only a few cents for several hundred. (Show the box with plain pick, and set them beside Johnnie.)

Once Johnnie was a part of a proud beautiful tree, but this tree was felled, sawed, split, and at last here is Johnnie Toothpick, a servant to pick people's teeth. But Johnnie is a very WILLING servant; he never complains about his tasks. Do you complain when you are asked to do the dishes, correct your math problems, put your books away, come in from recess, do homework or run errands at home?

Johnnie Toothpick does not have to do the same thing all the time. Sometimes he helps serve dinner. (Show the dish of pickle slices and place it beside Johnny on the serving table.) Serving dinner is often a very important task, particularly at Christmas, Thanksgiving, or when special guests are coming. If we learn the small ways to serve, obey willingly, we can serve in the more important places.

Now here is another way Johnny serves. (Show the toothpick swabs.) He often is used to soothe a wound. You too can help those who are in trouble.

Sometimes Johnny Toothpick is asked to serve in a big, beautiful way. Perhaps he serves at a banquet or party. (Show the grapefruit with gumdrop-covered picks.) If we are obedient (or faithful) in the small things at first, God will count us as faithful and give us greater things to do.

Betty Stubbs, *Bible Lessons for Boys and Girls,* 1954

More Resources on Character

The resources below may be used during the second week if you would like to include a story on a particular day. You may also choose to use some of these stories if you are only dealing with upper graders during the first week.

The first resource is from www.youtube.com. The first clip depicts a high school and medical school class. It is more appropriate for upper grades 5-8. http://www.youtube.com/watch?v =xDayDdxpw_M&feature=related. The clip below gives examples of honesty and includes a rap with the words—be honest. We always need to tell the truth. http://www.youtube.com/ watch?v=Fx4Kiq3G86U Even though this may appeal more to the younger students it is an example of what older students could create.

The second resource is http://www.values.com. You will find inspirational stories, quotations, and a list of character traits which they believe make a difference in communities. In addition they have podcasts, billboards, radio and TV spots. The TV spot below is a 60 second spot about honesty which you may have seen on TV. http://www.values.com/inspirational-stories-tv-spots/91-Classroom

Upper grade students could get an idea of how to build their own Wiki or power point, etc, about all the character traits to present at the end of the quarter or semester.

Another Internet resource is Mr. Henry's Wild and Wacky World. You can join Mr. Henry as he uses scripture references, Bible stories, games, and puzzles to discover the truth about various character traits. You will learn surprising lessons about God and His word when you join the never ending action that fills Mr. Henry's workshop. These are longer presentations, but you can use them as a continuing story. It is a little wacky so be sure to preview the presentations before you use them. Have Fun!!! http://www.youtube.com/playlist?list=PL9 A96710954DD6695

You may also choose to use **Kids of Integrity** http://www.kidsofintegrity.com.

You will find Bible stories, texts, object lessons, and a variety of other tools which are free.

As a faith-filled parent/teacher, you want to help your children develop Christ-like attitudes and behavior. But this important responsibility can seem overwhelming. How do you know where to start?

Kids of Integrity is a set of free resources that will help you coach your kids with confidence and a clear sense of direction. Better still, *Kids of Integrity* will excite your children about living "God's way."

Week Ten

Character

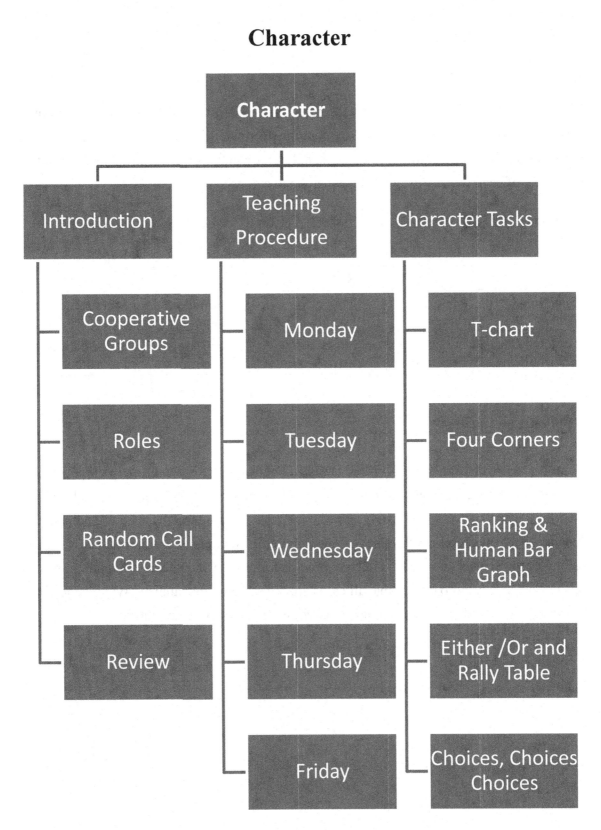

Cooperative Groups

Continue to reinforce the use of cooperative groups.

Roles

It is time to change roles. Remember, the persons in each group still keep the same number however now you change the roles. You continue to rotate through the roles each time you introduce a new character trait (see example below) or you may choose to change roles at the beginning of each week. Post the roles where they can be seen.

Week 1 & 2	Week 3 & 4	Week 5 & 6	Week 7 & 8	Week 9 & 10
Reporter 3	Reporter 2	Reporter 1	Reporter 4	Reporter 3
Recorder 4	Recorder 3	Recorder 2	Recorder 1	Recorder 4
Materials Person 1	Materials Person 4	Materials Person 3	Materials Person 2	Materials Person 1
Social Skills/ Environment 2	Social Skills/ Environment 1	Social Skills/ Environment 4	Social Skills/ Environment 3	Social Skills/ Environment 2

Random Call Cards

Continue to use the Random Call name cards and table cards for two primary purposes; one, for you to get better acquainted with the students, and second, as a means to call on them randomly when answers to questions or when reports on assignments need to be presented. As a teacher you need to always have your Random Call cards with you because randomly calling on participants is such an effective process for getting and keeping their attention. For this reason, you want to ensure that all cards are the same in appearance. Avoid using colors or marks that would help participants to discriminate their card from another.

Teaching Procedure Week 10

Monday

T-Chart

"Now let's use a T-chart to find out what **character** *'looks like'* and *'sounds like.'"* (Draw a T-chart as illustrated on the next page on chart paper or on your computer screen.) "What will a person say and do when they are showing **character**? Remember, I am looking for concrete, observable behavior, something that you can hear someone say or see what they do." (Divide groups as needed, i.e., half of the classroom will complete *"looks like"* and the other half *"sounds like"* or 1's and 3's complete *"looks like"* and 2's and 4's will complete *"sounds like,"* etc.)

"I will give you 3 minutes to work in your groups. Try to think of 3 or 4 examples. Then I will call on the reporters to give me the responses . . . Time is up. I will use my Random Call cards to decide which table will share first. Then we will continue by using a Round Robin" (See Appendix.) "Allowing each group an opportunity to share one example." Fill out the T-chart or invite a student who has good writing to fill it in as the teams share their suggestions.

After completing one round (meaning that each group has had a chance to contribute), you may choose to do another round or you may open the floor for any suggestions which have not yet been recorded. When finished, post the T-chart in the classroom.

"We will post the T-chart where we all can see it. If we think of other examples of what character *'looks like'* or *'sounds like'* during the week, we will add them to the T-chart."

T-Chart	

Character

Looks Like	Sounds Like

"Before we have prayer asking God to help us develop a good character, let's review the definition." You may have the entire class repeat it together, boys, then girls, different groups, etc. Remind them to practice all the **character** traits they are learning throughout the day and at home. Then finish with prayer.

Tuesday

Four Corners—You will need to write the name of 4 of the stories you used last week on 8 1/2 by 11 sheets of paper. You may use white or colored paper.

Why the Difference?	The Young Captain Who Stood His Ground	Frogs in the Cream	Johnnie Toothpick

"Good morning class!!! It's time for worship. I would like you to use a Think-square-share to discuss the **character attributes** you practiced yesterday or to discuss if you noticed anyone else who was practicing a specific **character** trait." (Give them from 30 seconds to 1 1/2 minutes to discuss.) "Now I will use my Random Call cards." (Call on 2-3 students and then open the floor.)

"Today we are going to use a Four Corners activity for our worship. You will notice the titles of 4 of the stories/activities we used for worship posted around the classroom, one on each wall. I want you to think of which story/activity was your favorite. Be sure to think of as many reasons for your choice as you can. Think individually. That's right; I should not hear any talking. Now that you have had time to think I want you to stand up and walk to the story/activity you chose. Once everyone is standing by the story/activity they chose, I want you to Turn-to-your-neighbor and talk about why you made the choice you did." (You will have to judge how much time they need, but do not give them too much time. Use the raising of your hand or whatever signal you use to get students' attention.)

"Now I will use Random Call cards. If I call your name then your group will begin (or you may begin with the corner that has the most people or least), and then we will continue around the classroom. We will use a Round Robin to call on each corner to give me one reason they heard or they presented . . . You have given some very good reasons. I will open the floor . . . Good work. You may go back to your seats."

Before prayer you may ask the following questions and have the entire class answer, or different groups, or individuals. "What's the word for this week? What is the definition? What is the text in the Bible that tells us we need to develop proper **character**? Excellent!!! You were able to tell me word for word the definition for **character** and the text in the Bible that tells us we need to develop proper **character**. Let's bow our heads for prayer as we ask God to help us to continue to develop proper **character**."

Wednesday

Ranking—You will need to have a copy of the exercise so each student can access the information and work individually to complete the task of ranking three or more tasks in their order of preference or priority.

"This morning we are going to complete a ranking exercise for worship. I would like the materials person to come and take enough of the materials for each person in your group. Each of you needs to answer the question individually. Let's read the question together:

When deciding about the character of someone else, what is most important to you?

_____ The way they make you feel

_____ What they think and talk about

_____ What they do

"Remember this is about what you think: 1 = most important; 2 = next important; 3 = next; I am going to give you 3 minutes to work individually. After you have completed the task, you may discuss your ranking with your group.

"To complete this exercise let's create a Human Bar Graph. I have three different pieces of paper on a wall/board with each paper having one of the choices written on it. Line up under your number one choice." (Students should be facing you so they form a bar graph. There are many connections you can help the students make at this time. Which has the most people? What can you learn from where people stood?) "Talk-to-your-neighbor and share why you made the choice you did for your number one." I will then call on some of you randomly. You can tell me what you said or what your neighbor said. Even though this is not math class, did you notice how much easier it is to see how the class voted?" Call on two or three and then open the floor to others who wish to respond.

"Excellent work!!! You were able to make a choice and explain why that choice was most important to you. You may return to your seat. Let's repeat the word, definition, and text before we have prayer today." Make any other observations that are appropriate to the lesson.

Thursday

Either/Or—You will need to write the words SHORT TIME/ LONG TIME on 8 1/2 by 11 sheets of paper. You may use white or colored paper. Post these on opposite sides of the room.

SHORT TIME	LONG TIME

"For worship today you will be able to participate in an Either/Or exercise. Remember that even though you may like both choices, you are forced to choose one and give your reasons for making that choice. Here is the question: For you does it take a short time or a long time to tell what a person's character is?

"Yes, you have to think first and I should hear no talking" (Give them time to think, perhaps 30 seconds.) "Now you may go to the side of your choice. Turn-to-your-neighbor and talk about why you made the choice you did." You will have to judge how much time they need, but do not give them too much time. Use the raising of your hand or whatever signal you use to get students' attention.

"We will use a Rally Table to share your thoughts. In a Rally Table one person from one side gives a reason then another person from the other side shares a reason. Let's begin with those of you who chose long time. Anyone in the group can give a reason they choose long time or a reason someone else in the group chose long time. Good, you were able to give a reason why it takes a long time to tell what a person's character is. Now let's go to the short time. Give me just one reason. Let's go back to long time. It is like playing tennis, you go back and forth." Continue until you stop the process. Share your choice at the end too.

"Well done. You were able to tell why you thought it takes a short time or a long time for you to tell a person's character. You may go back to your seats." Before prayer you could find out if they want to add anything else to the T-chart, make comments on those you have seen who have continued to build their character, etc.

135

Friday

Have each group illustrate **character**. Choices could include finding or creating:

1. Songs
    a. They can write their own words to a familiar tune or find a song
2. Find or create a story or speech
3. Skits/role play
4. Acronyms
5. Pictorials
6. Power Point presentation or other digital presentations
7. Videos they find or create or,
8. Combinations of these

"Remember, each person in the group has to be involved in the presentation. Have fun and make it memorable."

Special Note: Make this day special. Be creative!!!!!

Week Eleven & Twelve

Table of Contents

Week Eleven

Honesty

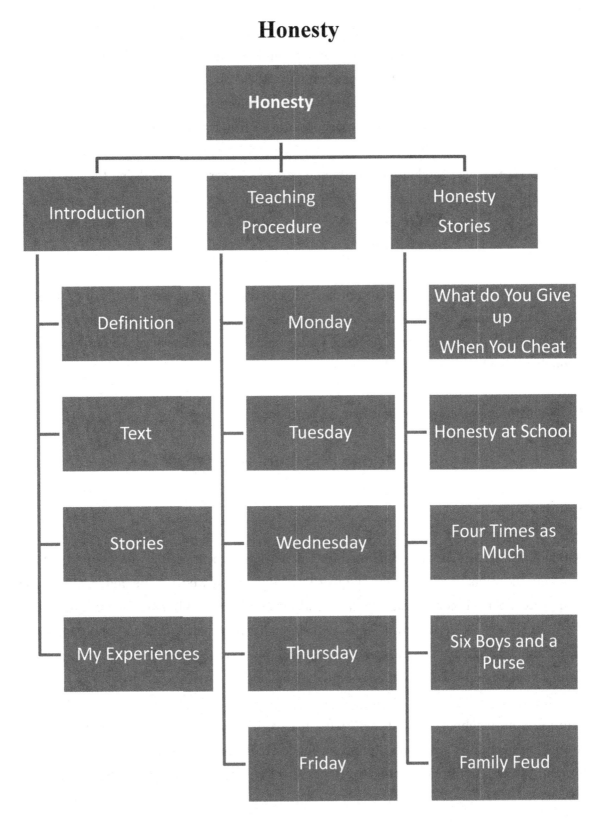

Honesty

Definition: Honesty is to be completely truthful, upright, and just.

Attributes: (1) Tell the truth; (2) To be correct or right; (3) To be fair.

Text: Proverbs 20:11—"Even a child is known by his behavior. His actions show if he is innocent and good."* ICB

Stories: At the end of the week you may ask students to write about their favorite story/object lesson from those that were shared during the week.

My Experiences: Students write about a personal experience involving the trait for the week. Students may take pictures and post, interview someone and post, prepare a short video, or other media enhanced method to present their experience.

You could also make a digital record of the word, definition, attributes, text, stories, and my experience and post it on the class webpage, wiki, or electronic notebook. However, it is imperative that you create a specific place for worship where students can see the information throughout the day.

* You may use another appropriate text if you choose.

Teaching Procedure Week 11

Monday

"Good morning. Let's review our word for last week by repeating the word, definition, and text from the Bible. Ready, begin. The word we studied last week is **character**. **Character** is the way a person feels, thinks, and acts and the text in the Bible that tells us how to feel, think, and act is Philippians 4:8—'Fix your thoughts on what is true and good and right. Think about things that are pure and lovely, and dwell on the fine, good things in others. Think about all you can praise God for and be glad about.'

"Turn-to-your-neighbor and tell them what the word is for this week. That's correct. The word is **honesty.** Let's read the definition together. **Honesty** is to be completely truthful, upright, and just. Let's read our text together using a complete sentence. The text in the Bible that tells us to be **honest** is Proverbs 20:1—'Even a child is known by his behavior. His actions show if he is innocent and good.'

Read: "Why the Difference" story or talk about weekend happenings. (p. 117)

Pray—"Let's ask God to help us be **honest**."

Tuesday

"It's time for worship. Oh! Look at how quickly everyone put their things away! Thank you for being so efficient. Everyone, on the count of three tell me the word we are studying this week. One, two, three" (honesty). "That's correct. I'm going to give you 2 minutes to learn the definition, but first let's all read it together—'Honesty is to be completely truthful, upright, and just.'

"Use a complete sentence to tell your neighbor the word we are studying this week" (Reply—"The word we are studying this week is **honesty**.") "Very good. Now use a complete sentence to repeat the definition of **honesty** to a different neighbor at your table." (I like the way Ken is turning to another neighbor to give the definition.)

Read: "Honesty at School" story. (p. 153)

Ask Questions: Use Think-square-share. For Share use Random Call cards and reporters.

1. Who was **honest** in this story? (Literal, Knowledge)
2. How were they **honest**? (Comprehension)
3. What happened because of their **honesty**? (Comprehension)
4. How will **honesty** help you? (Creative, Synthesis)
5. Do you think **honesty** is worthwhile? Why? (Evaluation, Critical)

(Answer for # 4 could include reputation, getting a job, getting and keeping friends, feeling good about oneself, etc.)

Pray: "Remember to ask God to help us develop honesty."

Wednesday

"Good morning. It's so good to be able to come in class and see people who are being efficient. Nancy, George—in fact this whole half of the class is being efficient. I've seen people who are persevering, obedient, and attentive. Now, I'd like to have everyone's full attention. That's correct. I need your eyes, ears, and heart, excellent!!! This Friday we are going to have an important review of the six words we have studied so far. I'm telling you so you may begin reviewing right away.

"Today is the day everyone recites the text by heart. I'm going to give you two minutes. (The text in the Bible that tells us to be honest is Proverbs 20:11—'Even a child is known by his behavior. His actions show if he is innocent and good.' After practicing by yourself for 1 minute, you may use a Round Robin to practice the verse. Ready, start.

"Who is ready? I see many hands." (Randomly call on one student. Let everyone try and give them all positive reinforcement. Remember the praise needs to be specific. For example, Jake, you were able to say the verse quickly and without any errors. Good work.)

Read: "Four Times as Much" story. (p. 150)

Ask Questions:

1. Who was **honest** in this story? (Literal, Knowledge)
2. How was the person **honest**? (Comprehension)
3. What do you think would have happened if he had used the money he saved? (Synthesis, Creative)
4. When should a person begin to pay tithe? (Interpretive, Application, Critical)

Pray: Ask God to help us develop **honesty.**

Thursday

"Good morning. I'd like everyone's attention. Thank you. This entire half of the class obeyed immediately and they are listening with their ears, eyes, and heart. Now everyone is listening, Congratulations!!! I hope you are reviewing because tomorrow will be our review game.

"Today is the day we are trying to say the word, the definition, and the text using a complete sentence and all without looking.

"I'll give you four minutes." (Change the amount of time as needed.) "Remember, everyone must use a complete sentence. Let's say it together. Our word for this week is **honesty**. **Honesty** is being completely truthful, upright, and just. The text in the Bible that tells us to develop honesty is Proverbs 20:11—'Even a child is known by his behavior. His actions show if he is innocent and good.' Practice individually for two minutes and then practice with your group.

"Who is ready to say it just like we practiced?" Let everyone try. Those who have difficulty, say, "You are doing it well and just need to study it a little bit more. I'll give you another chance tomorrow. Continue to persevere, you can do it. That's excellent," etc.

Read: "Six Boys and a Purse" story (p. 148)

Use Think-square-share and Random Call cards to answer the following questions:

1. Who was **honest** in this story? (Knowledge/Literal)
2. How was/were the person(s) **honest**? (Comprehension)
3. How can **honesty** help you? (Analysis, Interpretive)
4. Who has noticed a classmate who has been **honest**? Be sure to include in what ways they were **honest**. (Evaluation, Critical)

Pray: "Let's ask God to help us be **honest** in all that we do." (Remember to take every opportunity to use the word and comment on it.)

Friday

"Good morning, class!" (Remember, this is a special day!)

How to Make It a Special Day

Option 1:

1. Invite a visitor: pastor, vice-principal, academy teacher, parent, etc.
2. Use the Story Hour CDs and let the students decorate their papers to give away.
3. Let students sit with a friend.
4. Begin with the story "Attentiveness in the Bible" before doing anything else.
5. Use some academy students to present a skit.

Option 2: Family Feud:

Equipment Needed:

1. Teams (An even number of teams is needed—two, four, or six. If you have a small class, just divide them into two teams.)
2. Two desk bells.
3. Score keeper
4. Announcer
5. Judge

Playing the Game:

1. Each family (Team A and Team B) has their members stand in a predetermined order.
2. Each team has a desk bell.
3. Each team will receive four questions. Each question is worth two points except for the last question which is worth four points.
4. Each family or team has their first member step forward in front of a desk bell. One hand is ready to hit the bell and the other is behind his or her back.
5. Announcer asks the first question. The first person to hit the bell gets to answer the question. If he or she answers correctly the #2 player on the team may answer the #2 question. Then question #3 for #3 player, etc.

6. If one of the players doesn't give the correct answer, Team B or the other family is able to answer the question and receive points for it. This is called "a steal." Anyone on the team may be designated to answer the question when it is a steal.

7. After Family or Team A and B play, have family C and D play, etc.

The idea is to have fun and see how much they remember. Here are some questions you may use.

SUGGESTED QUESTIONS

1. Recite Matthew 19:23.
2. Name a story that shows perseverance in the Bible.
3. Give the definition for efficiency.
4. What are all these words that we are studying called?
5. Which character trait is one of the teacher's favorites?
6. Give the text and recite the verse that tells us to be obedient.
7. What word means to continue to do something in spite of difficulties or obstacles.
8. When Gideon chose men to fight for him, what characteristic did he use to make his choice?
9. Give the text that tells us to listen.
10. What is another word for listening?
11. Recite the text that tells us to be efficient.
12. Tell one way you were efficient at home.
13. In which definition does the word willingly appear?
14. Recite James 1:19.
15. Recite Ecclesiastes 9:10.
16. What is the only thing that we can take to heaven?
17. Mention a story that shows the importance of being efficient.
18. Define attentiveness.
19. Define obedience.
20. Give the first six words in the order we studied them.
21. What is character?
22. Define honesty.
23. What character trait does Proverbs 20:11 tell us about?
24. Recite Philippians 4:8.
25. What will help your reputation?

Option 3:

Divide the class into groups and have them create a review activity that can be used next week or the last week of the quarter. What can they do?

1. Word search
2. Jeopardy game
3. Wheel of Fortune (other games you choose)

Stories of Honesty

What Do You Give up When You Cheat?

In the school cafeteria, Seth gulped down his lunch without even tasting it. His mind was on the math assignment he had to finish and turn in next period. It was an open book test, but the teacher had said the students couldn't work together on the answers. Unfortunately, there was no way Seth could finish the test without help. He had an A in the class up to now, and he knew this assignment was going to pull his grade down.

As he scraped his chair away from the table and finally raised his head to look around the room, he saw three of his friends at a table in the back corner, their heads together, obviously working on some assignment. The open-book test?

Seth picked up his tray and walked to their table. "Whatcha doin?" he asked?

"Working on the test—what else?" one of his friends replied with a laugh.

"But we're not supposed to work together," Seth reminded then.

"Come on, Man," the boy said with a laugh. "If we don't work together, we won't get finished. But if he worked with them on it, he wouldn't feel right inside. What would you do?

It doesn't always feel good to do the right thing—not right away, at least. But there are always two consequences: short range and long range. The short range consequences of being honest may hurt a little. Seth didn't get his A but in the long run he felt better. He liked himself.

This "liking yourself" can be called "integrity" (honesty). You are not shaken, feeling guilty, wondering if you'll get found out, it is something to protect. It is what you lose when you cheat.

Integrity (honesty) is a gift from God. We can chip away at it bit by bit and feel awful, or we can take care of it and watch it grow. Will your integrity have grown or shrunk five years from now? Ten years? Fifty? It's up to you.

From *Daily Devotional: Out of this World*
by permission of Nancy Beck Irland

Six Boys and a Purse

Six boys were playing in a straw stack near a small town some distance to the north of us here. One of the boys found among the straw a purse with $2.20. All the boys became excited with the idea that there might be more money where that came from, so they set about exploring and searching among the straw, and sure enough, they found needs some more—$94.20 in cash and a check for $ 41.19.

They were really excited now. Should they keep the money and divide it among themselves? They did not! Instead, they hunted up the chief of police of the little town, told him the story, and returned the money and check over to him. The chief of police remembered that a man had reported to him some time before that he had lost some money at that straw stack, and the policeman set about to find the man.

What about the boys? The newspaper said: "In the meantime six boys have something ten thousand times more valuable than the money they found; they have the respect and self esteem of everybody in the neighborhood; a reputation for honesty that will bring them wealth and fame and honor if they just keep on as they have started."

This story appeared in the Mountain View, California, newspaper of March 31, 1993.

The Spelling Bee

Today is the spelling bee. Only three students had gone to the foot of the long line. The teacher put a very hard word to the student at the head of the line, and he missed, everyone down the line missed it until it came to the last student in line, who spelled it.

"Mary, you may go to the head of the class," and Mary happy with her success, went to the head of her class.

The teacher then wrote the more difficult word on the board, and as soon as Mary saw it she said, "Oh, Miss White! I didn't spell it that way."

Before the teacher could reply, Mary went back to the foot of the class, quicker than she had gone to the head. She was too honest to take credit for something she had not done.

She remembered that "Even a child is known by his doings."

From *A Child's Book of Character Building—Book 1*
by permission of Association of Christian Schools International

Four Times as Much

J ohn had been taught by his mother to give to God one tenth of all the money he earned. It is a noble thing to do, and the Bible says that people who follow this plan with their money may always be sure of receiving a special blessing from heaven.

From the very first time that John had earned any money of his own he had most carefully set aside one tenth for the Lord. This he had put in the collection plate at church. If he received ten cents for doing some gardening, then he saved one cent for God. If he received 50 cents for helping to wash somebody's car, then he put five cents aside in the same way.

Year by year as he grew older he continued to divide his money like this, but, by and by, as he saw many things that he wanted to buy like other boys at school, he began to leave God out sometimes. He didn't tell Mother, of course, because he knew that she would be disappointed; and so that he wouldn't feel bad about himself, he made a little note in a note book of all he knew he should pay and didn't. He told himself that someday, when he had made a great deal of money, he would pay it all up.

Of course that day did not come. It never comes. And so the figures in John's little notebook grew larger and larger, and the possibility of his ever paying it became more and more remote.

Then one day he came home from school all excited with the news that a very special outing was planned. His teacher had arranged for a wonderful trip into the country, where they would have boat rides and good things to eat, and what not. The only difficulty was the expense. It was going to cost three dollars each.

"Well," said Mother, "that settles it. I couldn't pay all that. If you want to go very badly, you will have to use some of your own money."

John's face fell. He did so want to go with all the others in his class, but how could he use any more of his money when he owed God so much money already?

Going upstairs, he opened the drawer where he kept his pennies and a little account book and began to count up to see how much he still had left.

Twenty-five cents, fifty cents, a dollar, one dollar fifty, one dollar seventy-five cents, two dollars.

So he counted.

"Two dollars and fifty cents, two dollars and seventy-five cents, three dollars."

He had enough, just enough. He could go to the outing after all!

But then he noticed the little notebook. Opening it slowly, he began counting again. And the more he counted, the more his heart sank.

Could it be possible he owed God so much?

One dollar, two dollars. Three dollars!

Dreadful thought! If he paid God all he owed Him he would have nothing left. Then he could not possibly go to the outing. What should he do?

He was getting into a terrible state of mind when the door opened softly and Mother entered. Quickly he threw his money and book into the drawer and closed it.

But somehow Mother guessed what was the matter. Mother always does guess right, doesn't she?

Sitting down on John's bed, Mother picked up his Bible and turned the pages slowly until she came to the third chapter of the book of Malachi. And there she read those familiar words: "Will a man rob God? Yet ye have robbed Me. But ye say, wherein have we robbed Thee? In tithes and offerings . . . . Bring ye all the tithes into the storehouse, that there may be meat in Mine house, and prove Me now herewith, saith the Lord of hosts, if I will not open you the windows of heaven and pour you out a blessing, that there shall not be room enough to receive it."

John had heard Mother read these verses many times before, but somehow this time they made a deeper impression on his mind than ever before.

"Mother," he said, "I've decided not to go to that outing."

"You have, dear?" said Mother. "Why?"

"Well, I might as well tell you. I have just three dollars saved up, and I owe it all to God. I haven't paid my tithe since I don't know when and I'm going to pay it now instead of going on the outing. I wish you would take this money, so that I won't be tempted to spend it."

John passed over his precious three dollars to Mother, who, for a moment, hardly knew what to say.

"I think," she said after a pause, "you have made the right decision, John, and I am sure that somehow it will come out right. God does such wonderful things, you know, when we try to please Him. And when He opens the windows of heaven, He usually opens them wide."

The next few days were hard for John. It seemed as though every few minutes some boy or girl would ask him whether he was going on the outing, and he would have to reply, No, not this time, thank you." And then he would be asked, "Why not? What's the matter? Are you sick? Is your mother ill? Don't you like outings?" and he would try to explain without really telling them anything.

At last the outing day arrived. This, thought John, would be the hardest day of all—to see everybody going away, and have to stay behind himself.

And then, early that morning, the postman called. He had a letter for John. It was from a relative living in the West Indies. Inside was a check for twelve dollars—exactly four times as much as the tithe John had given to God. John went to the outing after all. Indeed, he was the happiest boy there. The windows of heaven had opened again.

From *Uncle Arthur's Bedtime Stories*
by permission of Review and Herald

Honesty at School

" I am happy to announce that the winner of the art contest is Juan Cortez!" reported Mr. Higdon, the principal.

It can't be true, Juan thought. I rushed to complete my picture. It can't be good enough to win.

As Mr. Higdon shook Juan's hand, he proudly pointed to Juan's prize-winning painting. Juan's eyes grew as big as golf balls. The picture to which Mr. Higdon pointed was not his. It really belonged to Bentley Brown.

Many questions ran through Juan's mind: What shall I do? Why was my name on the picture? How did it happen? Everyone knows that Bentley is the best artist in the class. There are students in the class who do not like Bentley. I wonder if they switched my name with his, so that he wouldn't win.

Juan had always been truthful in his words and ways. That was being like Jesus. Now he had the opportunity to show others that being honest was more important to him than winning the contest. Motioning to Mr. Higdon, he whispered the truth in the principal's ear.

"Thank you, Juan, for being so honest," said Mr. Higdon. "I will correct the mistake right now."

Juan felt a little disappointed as he handed the winner's ribbon to Bentley Brown. But he was sure that he had made the right decision. He knew he had pleased Jesus, too.

From *A Child's Book of Character Building—Book 1*
by permission of Association of Christian Schools International

More Resources on Honesty

The resources below may be used during the second week if you would like to include a story on a particular day. You may also choose to use some of these stories if you are only dealing with upper graders during the first week.

The first resource is from www.youtube.com The first clip depicts a high school and medical school class. It is more appropriate for upper grades 5-8. http://www.youtube.com/watch?v =xDayDdxpw_M&feature=related. The clip below gives examples of honesty and includes a rap with the words—be honest. We always need to tell the truth. http://www.youtube.com/ watch?v=Fx4Kiq3G86U Even though this may appeal more to the younger students it is an example of what older students could create.

The second resource is http://www.values.com. You will find inspirational stories, quotations, and a list of character traits which they believe make a difference in communities. In addition they have podcasts, billboards, radio and TV spots. The TV spot below is a 60 second spot about honesty which you may have seen on TV.

http://www.values.com/inspirational-stories-tv-spots/91-Classroom

Upper grade students could get an idea of how to build their own Wiki or power point, etc, about all the character traits to present at the end of the quarter or semester.

Another Internet resource is Mr. Henry's Wild and Wacky World. You can join Mr. Henry as he uses scripture references, Bible stories, games, and puzzles to discover the truth about various character traits. You will learn surprising lessons about God and His word when you join the never ending action that fills Mr. Henry's workshop. These are longer presentations, but you can use them as a continuing story. It is a little wacky so be sure to preview the presentations before you use them. Have Fun!!! http://www.youtube.com/playlist?list=PL9 A96710954DD6695

You may also choose to use **Kids of Integrity** http://www.kidsofintegrity.com/honesty. You will find Bible stories, texts, object lessons, and a variety of other tools which are free.

As a faith-filled parent/teacher, you want to help your children develop Christ-like attitudes and behavior. But this important responsibility can seem overwhelming. How do you know where to start?

Kids of Integrity is a set of free resources that will help you coach your kids with confidence and a clear sense of direction. Better still, *Kids of Integrity* will excite your children about living "God's way."

Week Twelve

Honesty

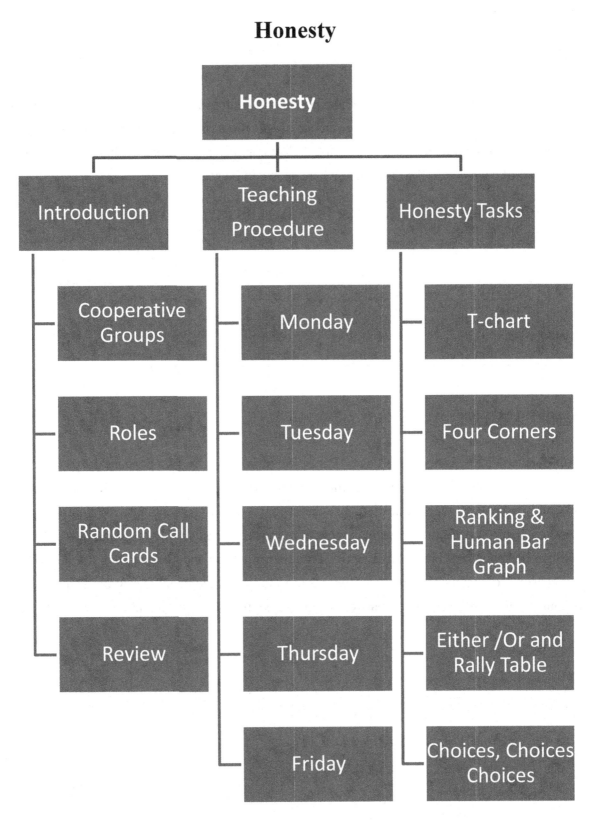

Cooperative Groups

Continue to reinforce the use of cooperative groups.

Roles

It is time to change roles. Remember, the persons in each group still keep the same number however now you change the roles. You continue to rotate through the roles each time you introduce a new character trait (see example below) or you may choose to change roles at the beginning of each week. Post the roles where they can be seen.

Week 11 & 12	Week 13 & 14	Week 15 & 16	Week 17 & 18
Reporter 3	Reporter 2	Reporter 1	Reporter 4
Recorder 4	Recorder 3	Recorder 2	Recorder 1
Materials Person 1	Materials Person 4	Materials Person 3	Materials Person 2
Social Skills/ Environment 2	Social Skills/ Environment 1	Social Skills/ Environment 4	Social Skills/ Environment 3

Random Call Cards

Continue to use the Random Call name cards and table cards for two primary purposes; one, for you to get better acquainted with the students, and second, as a means to call on them randomly when answers to questions or when reports on assignments need to be presented. As a teacher you need to always have your Random Call cards with you because randomly calling on participants is such an effective process for getting and keeping their attention. For this reason, you want to ensure that all cards are the same in appearance. Avoid using colors or marks that would help participants to discriminate their card from another.

Teaching Procedure Week 12

Monday

T-Chart

"Now let's use a T-chart to find out what **honesty** '*looks like*' and '*sounds like.*'" (Draw a T-chart as illustrated on the next page on chart paper or on your computer screen.) "What will a person say and do when they are showing **honesty**? Remember, I am looking for concrete, observable behavior, something that you can hear someone say or see what they do." (Divide groups as needed, i.e., half of the classroom will complete *"looks like"* and the other half *"sounds like"* or 1's and 3's complete *"looks like"* 2's and 4's will complete *"sounds like"* etc.)

"I will give you 3 minutes to work in your groups. Try to think of 3 or 4 examples. Then I will call on the reporters to give me the responses . . . Time is up. I will use my Random Call cards to decide which table will share first. Then we will continue by using a Round Robin" (See Appendix.) "Allowing each group an opportunity to share one example." (Fill out the T-chart or invite a student who has good writing to fill it in as the teams share their suggestions.)

After completing one round (meaning that each group has had a chance to contribute), you may choose to do another round or you may open the floor for any suggestions which have not yet been recorded. When finished, post the T-chart in the classroom.

"We will post the T-chart where we all can see it. If we think of other examples of what honesty '*looks like*' or '*sounds like*' during the week, we will add them to the T-chart."

T-Chart

Honesty

Looks Like	Sounds Like

"Before we have prayer asking God to help us practice **honesty**, let's review the definition." You may have the entire class repeat it together, boys, then girls, different groups, etc. Remind them to practice being **honesty** throughout the day and at home. Then finish with prayer.

Tuesday

Four Corners—You will need to write the name of 4 of the stories read about **honesty** on 8 1/2 by 11 sheets of paper. You may use white or colored paper.

What Do You Give up When You Cheat?	Honesty at School	Four Times as Much	Six Boys and a Purse

"Today we are going to use a Four Corners activity for our worship. You will notice the titles of 4 of the stories we read last week about **honesty** posted around the classroom, one on each wall. I want you to think of which story was your favorite story about **honesty.** Be sure to think of as many reasons for your choice as you can. Think individually. That's right; I should not hear any talking. Now that you have had time to think I want you to stand up and walk to the title you chose. Once everyone is standing by the title they chose, I want you to Turn-to-your-neighbor and talk about why you made the choice you did." (You will have to judge how much time they need, but do not give them too much time. Use the raising of your hand or whatever signal you use to get students' attention.)

"Now I will use Random Call cards. If I call your name then your group will begin" (or you may begin with the corner that has the most people or least), "and then we will continue around the classroom. We will use a Round Robin to call on each corner to give me one reason they heard or they presented . . . You have given some very good reasons. I will open the floor . . . Good work. You may go back to your seats."

Before prayer you may ask the following questions and have the entire class answer, or different groups, or individuals. "What's the word for this week? What is the definition? What is the text in the Bible that tells us we need to be **honest**? Excellent!! You were able to tell me word for word the definition of **honesty** and the text in the Bible that tells us we need to develop honesty. Let's bow our heads for prayer as we ask God to help us to be **honest**."

Wednesday

Ranking—You will need to have a copy of the exercise so each student can access the information and work individually to complete the task of ranking three or more tasks in their order of preference or priority.

"This morning we are going to complete a ranking exercise for worship. I would like the materials person to come and take enough of the materials for each person in your group. Each of you needs to answer the question individually. Let's read the question together:

Being honest at all times is most helpful to:

_____ You

_____ God

_____ Others

_____ Your Teacher

"Remember this is about what you think: 1 = most important; 2 = next important; 3 = next; and 4 is least important. I am going to give you 3 minutes to work individually. After you have completed the task, you may discuss your ranking with your group.

"To complete this exercise let's create a Human Bar Graph. I have four different pieces of paper on a wall/board with each paper having one of the choices written on it. Line up under your number one choice." (Students should be facing you so they form a bar graph. There are many connections you can help the students make at this time. Which has the most people? What can you learn from where people stood?) "Talk-to-your-neighbor and share why you made the choice you did for your number one. I will then call on some of you randomly. You can tell me what you said or what your neighbor said." Call on two or three and then open the floor to others who wish to respond.

"Excellent work!!! You were able to make a choice and explain why that choice was most important to you. You may return to your seat. Let's repeat the word, definition, and text before we have prayer today."

Thursday

Either/Or—You will need to write the words OTHERS/ YOU on 8 1/2 by 11 sheets of paper. You may use white or colored paper. Post these on opposite sides of the room.

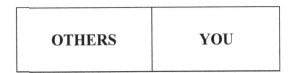

"For worship today you will be able to participate in an Either/Or exercise. It is one of my favorites. It is like the Four Corners exercise we did on Monday, except that in an Either/Or exercise you only have two choices. Even though you may like both choices, you are forced to choose one and give your reasons for making that choice. Here is the question: Being honest most helps you or others?

"We will use a Rally Table to share your thoughts. In a Rally Table one person from one side gives a reason then another person from the other side shares a reason. Let's begin with those of you who chose others. Anyone in the group can give a reason they chose others or a reason someone else in the group chose others. Good, you were able to give a reason why honesty is more helpful to you than others. Now let's go to you. Give me just one reason. Let's go back to others. It is like playing tennis, you go back and forth." (Ask one or two more and then open the floor. Share your choice at the end too.)

"Well done. You were able to tell why being honest most helps you or others. You may go back to your seats." (Before prayer you could find out if they want to add anything else to the T-chart, make comments on those you have seen who have continued to build their character, etc.)

Friday

Have each group illustrate **honesty**. Choices could include what they can find or create:

1. Songs/rap
    a. They can write their own words to a familiar tune or find a song
2. Find or create a story or speech
3. Skits/role play
4. Acronyms
5. Pictorials
6. Power Point presentation or other digital presentations
7. Videos they find or create or,
8. Combinations of these

"Remember, each person in the group has to be involved in the presentation. Have fun and make it memorable."

Special Note: Make this day special. Be creative!!!!!

Week Thirteen & Fourteen

Table of Contents

Week Thirteen

Kindness

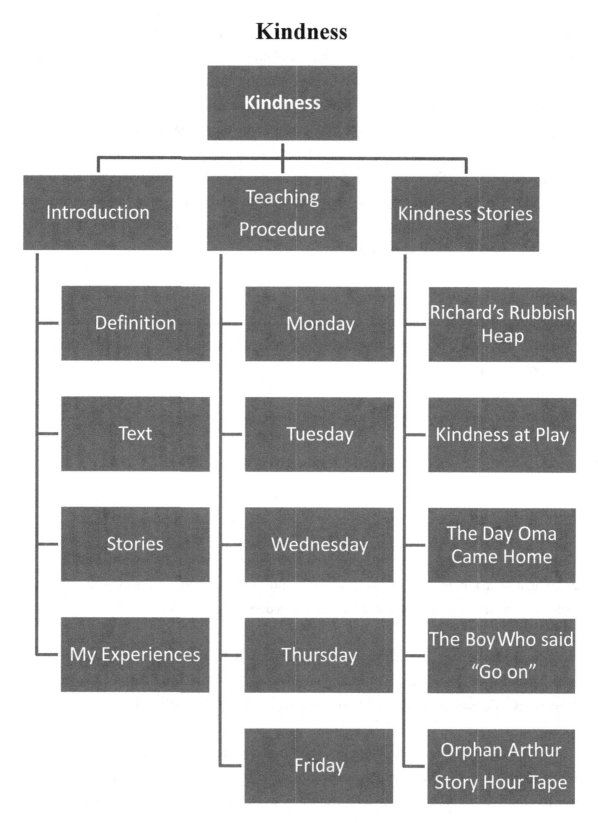

Kindness

Definition: A pleasant, generous, considerate, and friendly action.

Attributes: An action that is (1) Helpful; (2) Gentle; (3) Friendly.

Text: Ephesians 4:32—"Be kind and loving to each other. Forgive each other just as God forgave you in Christ." * ICB

Stories: At the end of the week you may ask students to write about their favorite story/object lesson from those that were shared during the week.

My Experiences: Students write about a personal experience involving the trait for the week. Students may take pictures and post, interview someone and post, prepare a short video, or other media enhanced method to present their experience.

You could also make a digital record of the word, definition, attributes, text, stories, and my experience and post it on the class webpage, wiki, or electronic notebook. However, it is imperative that you create a specific place for worship where students can see the information throughout the day.

* You may use another appropriate text if you choose.

Teaching Procedure Week 13

Monday

"Good morning. We have been studying so many important words these last six weeks. You are doing a great job developing these qualities and character traits. I like the way you are all learning to be attentive. Right now I can see everyone's eyes. Thank you.

"Turn-to-your-neighbor and tell them what the word is for this week. That's correct. The word is **kindness.** Let's read together the meaning of the word **kindness** using a complete sentence. **Kindness** is a pleasant, generous, considerate, and friendly action.

"The text in the Bible that encourages us to be **kind** is Ephesians 4:32. Let's read it together: 'Be ye kind one to another, tenderhearted, forgiving one another, even as God for Christ's sake has forgiven you.' Excellent, let's work this week on developing **kindness.**"

Talk about the weekend or read the story "Richard's Rubbish Heap." (p. 174)

Pray—"When we pray, let's ask God to help us develop **kindness**."

Tuesday

"Good morning, class! Use a complete sentence to tell your neighbor the word we are studying this week" (Reply—"The word we are studying this week is **kindness.**") "Very good.

"I'm going to give you three minutes to learn the word and definition." (Wait three minutes.) "Turn-to-your-neighbor and repeat the word and definition. Use Random Call cards to call on students. (Reply—"**Kindness** is a pleasant, generous, considerate, and friendly action." Make sure everyone has a turn and praise them. Remember to be specific with your praise.

"All of you did such a good job. Let's all say it together." (Reply—"The word we are studying this week is **kindness**. **Kindness** is a pleasant, generous, considerate, and friendly action.")

Read: "Kindness at Play" story. (p. 177)

"Next we will use a structure called Think-square-share. I want you to think individually about the answers to the questions about the story." (Give students time to think and then continue.) "You may now square with your group and discuss your responses. The recorder will write and reporter will report. Social skills persons, make sure all are involved in squaring."

Ask Questions: Use Think-pair-share. Use Random Call cards for sharing.

1. Who was **kind** in this story? (Literal, Knowledge)
2. How did he/she/they show **kindness** in this story? (Comprehension)
3. How did **kindness** make a difference in this story? (Application, Analysis)
4. Tell me at least one time when you showed **kindness** at school or at home. (Synthesis, Creative).

Call on different groups (tables, perhaps two) to report—they can each give one example and then open the floor.

"Your assignment is to observe when your classmates or you are practicing **kindness**. We will talk about it again tomorrow."

Challenge students: "I want you to find some way of practicing **kindness** at home this week. Be ready to share it with us on Friday." (TEACHER: Don't be afraid to use personal examples. They need a model. Example—"This morning I was **kind** when I . . . or I practiced **kindness** when I . . .")

Pray: Remind students to include the character trait they are working on.

Wednesday

"Good morning, class. This morning, let's say the word and the definition of the word we have been studying without looking at the board. Let's try it. Remember, we must use a complete sentence." (Reply—"The word we are studying this week is **kindness**, and the definition of the word **kindness** is a pleasant, generous, considerate, and friendly action.")

"Today, it's going to be harder. I'm going to give you three minutes to learn the verse. Remember you must use a complete sentence." You'll need to say, "The text in the Bible that helps us to be **kind** is Ephesians 4:32—'Be kind and loving to each other. Forgive each other just as God forgave you in Christ.' Practice in your head for 1 minute. Then use a Round Robin or Turn-to-your-neighbor and continue to practice the verse. I will tell you when you can begin to practice with others. Ready, start." (After one minute, give them the signal to practice with others if they wish.)

"Who is ready? I see many hands." (Randomly call on one student. Let everyone try and give them all positive reinforcement. Remember the praise needs to be specific. For example, Bill, you were willing and able to say the verse first and without any errors. Good work.)

Read: "The Day Oma Came Home" story (p. 178).

Ask Questions: Use Think-pair-share. Use Random Call cards to share.

1. Who was **kind** in the story? (Literal, Knowledge)
2. In what ways was he/she/they **kind**? (Comprehension)
3. How did **kindness** make a difference in this story? In what ways? (Analysis)

Pray: Always include something about **kindness**.

Teacher: During the day, always comment on those who are practicing **kindness**.

Thursday

"Good morning, class! Are you ready to tell us about kindness? Today is the day to say the word, the definition, and the text using a complete sentence without looking.

"I'll give you four minutes to review the word, definition, and text." (Change the amount of time as needed.) "I will be practicing too. Remember you must use a complete sentence. Let's read it together first. The word we are studying this week is **kindness. Kindness** is a pleasant, generous, considerate, and friendly action and the text in the Bible that tells us to be kind is Ephesians 4:32—'Be kind and loving to each other. Forgive each other just as God forgave you in Christ.' You may practice with a neighbor.'

"Let me try." (Go ahead and say it). "Who is ready to say it just as I did?" Let everyone try. Those who have difficulty, say, "I'll give you another chance tomorrow. Continue to persevere, you can do it."

Read: "The Boy Who Said, 'Go On'" story. (p. 181)

Use a Think-square-share to answer the following questions:

1. Who was **kind** in this story? (Literal, Knowledge)
2. How was the person **kind**? (Comprehension)
3. How can **kindness** help you be a better student? (Analysis)
4. Who has noticed a classmate who has been **kind**? Be sure to include in what ways they were **kind**. (Evaluation, Critical)

Pray: Thank God for giving us examples about kindness to follow.

Friday

"Good morning, class!" (Remember, this is a special day!)

How to Make It a Special Day

Option 1

1. Have a visitor: pastor, vice-principal, academy teacher, parent, etc.
2. Use the Story Hour tapes and let the students decorate their papers to give away.
3. Let students sit with a friend.
4. Use some academy students to give a skit.

Option 2

1. Use Story Hour CD "Orphan Arthur." It is in Book 8. It is excellent!!!
2. Let students finish the project that they started last week for review.

Option 3

Read "The Dog That Didn't Bite" before doing anything else. (This is more appropriate for older students.)

Repeat the word, definition, and text all together first. Remember to have anyone who did not say it the day before, say it today.

"Today all of you need to show me where you have written the word, text, definition, stories, and your experience on paper just as I have it on the board. Under stories, write one of the stories you remember that we discussed this week, telling how the person was **kind**" (Knowledge, Comprehension). "Under experience, write what you did to be **kind** here or at home" (Application). "You may also write the definition and text on another piece of paper and decorate it" (Knowledge, Creativity). "You could give this to one of your parents or another teacher. Who else might enjoy these?" (School staff, lay church members, etc.)

Students may begin writing these as early as Monday but save the decorating of the paper for Friday. You just want them to make a notebook or portfolio. These may be both paper and ink or electronic. Be sure they keep a list of the words so they can review them later.

Special Note: Make this day special. Be creative!!!!!

Pray: "Ask God to help us to remember the character traits we've learned."

Stories of Kindness

Richard's Rubbish Heap

Richard was as excited as a dog with ten tails. He had always wanted to "invent" something and now he had done so. His big "fire balloon," on which he had been working on for several weeks, was almost ready. There were just a few more odds and ends to fix, and then he would be able to set light to the wad of cotton set in a frame at the bottom and watch the big paper bag filled with hot air soar away into the sky.

It was going to be a big day for him, for all his friends were coming to see the great sight. He had told them all about it long before he had even worked out the design, and he was sure their eyes would "pop out" when they saw it completed.

And it was something else; too, I can tell you. Six feet high and four feet in diameter, it had been no small job to build. Richard had first made a framework of very strong wire. Then he had cut long strips of tissue paper, of various colors, all of the proper shape—like slices of orange peel so that when pasted together they made a big paper globe around the wire frame. What a task it had been pasting the edges of that paper!

At the very bottom of the frame there was a circle of wire in the center of which, supported on two cross wires, was the pad of cotton soaked in fuel, which, at the right moment, was to be set alight to heat the air inside the balloon. At last everything was ready for the grand ascent. All Richard's friends were standing around, waiting impatiently for the moment when the balloon would sail aloft.

Richard, however, was not in a hurry. He wanted to enjoy this moment of triumph to which he had looked forward to so long and for which he had worked so hard. He kept explaining how he had designed the balloon and why he was sure it would rise into the air. Over and over again he answered all the questions the boys asked about it.

At last, with a great flourish, he applied a match to the cotton. It flared up, and the children stood to the back to watch as the air inside became heated and the big tissue-paper bag gradually filled out.

"It's lifting!" cried Richard excitedly. "It's lifting! It's going up!"

He was clapping his hands for glee when a puff of wind blew the flame toward the tissue paper. There was no time to save it. In a moment, the whole balloon had dropped to the ground in flames.

Poor Richard! Heartbroken, he ran indoors, eager to get away from his friends who had expected so much of him and his much advertised "invention." He felt ashamed that he had said so much about it before it had been proved a success. And there was all the work he had put on it-all his spare time for weeks! Now there was nothing left but a heap of ashes and tangled wire.

That night Father found him in the bedroom. "Oh, why did it have to burn up?" moaned Richard.

"Don't worry too much about it," said Father. "Much worse things happen in this old world. What really matters is not that the old balloon is all burned up but that you worked so hard trying to make something worthwhile."

"But it's all wasted," wailed Richard.

"No, not wasted," said Daddy. "Think of all you have learned-all that you have read about balloons, all the little tricks about bending wire and sticking tissue paper together. All that isn't lost. It will prove useful someday. You'll see."

"But I so wanted to invent something," said Richard.

"I know," said Father, "but worthwhile things don't get invented as quickly as that. Think of Edison and how long he experimented before he invented the electric light and the phonograph and other things he gave the world. Do you think he discovered them all at once? No, indeed. He worked and worked over them, trying and failing and trying again."

"For weeks and weeks as I did?" asked Richard.

"Yes, for years and years" comforted Father. "And he had so many failures that it is a wonder he carried on as he did. You should just see his rubbish heap."

"His rubbish heap?" questioned Richard in surprise.

"Yes, indeed," said Father. "I've heard it is shown to all who visit one of his workshops. Every time an experiment went wrong, he would throw it out and start again. He didn't let failure discourage him, and neither must you. Build another balloon and a better one next time. Invent one that won't catch fire. Find out what was wrong and make it right. That's how all worthwhile inventions come about.

"I suppose that if Edison had a rubbish heap I shouldn't worry too much about my little pile of ashes," said Richard. "I'm going to start on a new balloon tomorrow."

"That's right," agreed Father. "That's the spirit that wins. Every real inventor has a rubbish heap, and you've made a good start toward success tonight."

(When you finish asking the questions of who was kind, also ask about the other trait perseverance—displayed at the end by Richard. Emphasize the idea of trying and failing and trying again. Those students who are having a hard time in certain subjects are often inspired by stories like this.)

From *Uncle Arthur's Bedtime Stories*
by permission of Review and Herald

Kindness at Play

"It must be tough for Ike to sit all day in that wheelchair," said Tommy as his neighborhood soccer team passed Ike's house.

"Why can't he walk?" asked Joey.

"Before you moved here, Ike hurt himself while diving into a swimming pool," Tommy said.

The boys walked on toward the soccer field. Tommy looked back at Ike. He could see a frown on his face. Ike was sad that he had no one to play with.

Tommy remembered last summer, when his leg was in a cast. He could not run or play, so he had to learn to play quiet games, such as checkers.

Maybe Ike would like to play checkers, thought Tommy. Then Tommy said, "Joey, you and the boys go play soccer, I am going to play with Ike."

Tommy went to Ike's house. "Hi Ike," said Tommy. "How would you like to play checkers?"

"Boy, would I!" said Ike, as Tommy came up the porch steps. "I was hoping that someone would play with me."

Tommy felt good inside, because he understood Ike's loneliness. Being kind, he was strong enough to make the right choice.

From *A Child's Book of Character Building—Book 1*
by permission of Christian Schools International

The Day Oma Came Home

Oma was Kim, Kari, and Kevin's grandmother.

Oma had been very sick. She had to spend many weeks in the hospital. But today she was coming home. She wasn't going to her own house. She was going to Kim, Kari and Kevin's house to live until she was stronger.

"Where do you think Oma should sleep?" Mommy asked the children.

"Your bed us the biggest," said Kim. "Maybe she could sleep with you and daddy."

"I don't think that would work," said Mommy. "Oma needs a bed of her own."

"She can sleep in my bed," said Kim, "and I could sleep with Kari."

"But you and Kari always fight over the covers and kick each other out of bed when you try to sleep together. And besides, I don't think Oma could climb up the ladder to your top bunk bed."

"She can sleep in my room," said Kevin.

"That's the best idea I've heard so far," said Mommy. We could move Kevin's crib and clothes and toys into Kim and Kari's bedroom and move the extra bed that is stored in the garage into Kevin's room, for Oma."

"That's a good idea," echoed the children. "When will Oma be here?"

"Soon," said Mommy, starting to push Kevin's crib through the door.

"May I help you?" asked Kim.

"Yes," said Mommy. "Help me guide the other end of this crib through the door."

"What can I do?" asked Kari.

"You may start bringing in Kevin's clothes and hanging them up in one side of your closet."

"Me too," said Kevin.

"Ok Kevin. You can move your toys from the toy shelf in your room to the toy shelf in Kim and Kari's room."

The children carried load after load from Kevin's room into Kim and Kari's room. Finally, Kevin's room was empty, and the other room was full.

"When will Oma be here?"

"Soon," said Mommy, moving the extra bed from the garage into Oma's new room.

"What else can we do?" asked the children.

"Kim, you can get a pitcher of cold water and a clean glass."

"Kari, you can cut some flowers and put them in a vase."

"Kevin, you can help me make this bed for Oma."

Just as the children finished their jobs, they heard a car in the driveway.

"Oma's here," they shouted as they rushed to greet her.

"Hi, Oma, you get to sleep in Kevin's room," they shouted.

"I put a pitcher of water by your bed," said Kim.

"And I picked some beautiful flowers for your room," said Kari.

"I made your bed," said Kevin.

Daddy helped Oma into the wheelchair towards the house, while Kevin got a free ride.

"What a pretty room!" Oma exclaimed. "Is this room just for me?"

"Yes," said Kim. "Kevin gets to sleep in our room."

"I'm a big boy now," said Kevin.

"It's going to be some fun sleeping in one room," said Kari.

Soon bedtime came. Oma was very tired. Kim gave her a drink of water. Kari put her glasses on the table by the flowers. And Kevin pulled down the covers on her bed and crawled in.

"I'm just warming up Oma's bed," said Kevin.

After Oma was tucked into the bed beside Kevin, Kari crawled in. "I just want to give Oma a back rub," said Kari.

And then Kim crawled in. "I just want to tell Oma a bedtime story," said Kim.

And by the time Mommy finished washing he supper dishes and Daddy finished feeding the dogs, what do you think they found when they looked n Oma's room?

There was Kevin,

    and Kari,

       and Kim,

           and Oma, all sound asleep in one bed.

From *Kim, Kari, and Kevin Storybook*
by permission of Kay Kuzma

The Boy Who Said "Go On"

Perhaps it was the noise, or the crowds of people, or the dozens and dozens of streets, leading in all directions that had bewildered the poor cat. Anyway, she was lost.

Thinking that perhaps id she were to cross the street she might find her way back home, she made a drive into the traffic, dodging here and there and doing her very best to het to the other side. But it was all too much for her. She felt as if she had become a mouse, and all these huge machines were chasing her, determined to kill her if possible.

"Oh, wow! What a close call that was!"

The wheel of a bus almost grazed her nose.

Phew! A taxicab dashed past, nearly shaving off her whiskers. Would she ever get across? Death seemed very near, and nobody seemed to care. She looked this way and that, not knowing whether to go forward or backward, and meanwhile she was sure another bus was coming straight toward her. Something was shouting, "Get out of the way!" and someone else, "Mind that cat!"

Then suddenly, when almost under the hood of the bus, a little ragged figure jumped toward her, picked her up in his strong arms, and leaped back in a flash onto the pavement.

It was only a poor newspaper boy, but she felt loved from him very much for his great kindness. No one else had thought of helping her desperate need.

He placed her gently on the pavement, and she purred contentedly.

Just then a big man came up to the boy. He looked as if he must be a lord, or at least a member of Parliament.

"That was a very brave deed, my boy," said he. "I would like you to give me your name and address for you deserve a medal for this."

"Go on!" said the boy.

"I really mean it," said the big gentleman. "Wouldn't you like a medal?"

"Go on!" repeated the lad. "Mother told us we had to be kind to animals, and not to expect any reward."

And with that the boy turned and bolted, leaving the big gentleman and the poor cat to stare at each other in surprise!

From *Uncle Arthur's Bedtime Stories*
by permission of Review and Herald

The Dog That Didn't Bite

The city-slicker had just driven up to the country store. He noticed a group of men sitting on one side of the store's porch engaged in a game of checkers. On the other side of the porch was a fellow sitting in a rocking chair.

The city-slicker, who was at the store to make a big sale and turn over a nice profit, decide that he would go over and speak to the man in the chair. The man had an old hound dog lying on the floor beside him. The city-slicker, knowing something of the love that country people had for their dogs, decided that the way to impress the man in the chair was to be nice to the man's dog. So he walked over to where the man was sitting.

"Howdy, mister," the city-slicker said. "Does your dog bite?" He asked. "Nope," replied the man. The city-slicker reached down to pet the dog on the head. The dog responded by biting the man's hand. Finally, when the other men managed to get the dog off the city-slicker, he spoke to the man in the chair again.

"I thought you said that your dog didn't bite," the city-slicker said. The country fellow still sitting in his chair, answered him. "My dog don't bite. That ain't my dog."

One of the tragedies of our age is our unwillingness to be helpful when we can. We see people who are headed for trouble, people whom we could be helpful to, and we simply make no effort to assist them. The Italian poet Dante once had this to say about such people: "He who sees the need and waits to be asked for help is unkind as if he had refused it."

Our generation is seemingly being influenced heavily by this policy of noninvolvement. We see places where we could help, where our help is needed, and we turn away with the thought that "that is none of our business." And that thought, that attitude, is totally false. If you can be of help to your fellowman, and he needs your help, then it is some of your business. We are all part of the family of man, and that makes us brothers.

Our reason for being in the world is to make a difference, to make it matter that we are here. And the finest way we can do that is to lend assistance where and when we can.

To have an opportunity to do good, and to fail to take advantage of that opportunity, is a reflection of a tragic flaw in our moral character. Non-involvement is a self-defeating attitude because the time will come, for each of us, when we ourselves will need tje assistance of another.

The Apostle Paul once wrote: "Be kind to one another . . ." That is still good sound advice today. And the Carpenter himself said: "Treat others as you would want them to treat you," in other words, if it isn't your dog, tell the man so!

Taken from *Words of Gold* by Donald E. Wildmon
by permission of Association of Christian Schools International.

More Resources on Kindness

T he resources below may be used during the second week if you would like to include a story on a particular day. You may also choose to use some of these stories if you are only dealing with upper graders during the first week.

The first resource is from www.youtube.com. The first clip describes a project about kindness. It describes the development and execution. This may be more appropriate for upper graders. http://www.youtube.com/watch?feature=endscreen&NR=1&v=7XFrNd0RuJ0. The clip below talks about what nice means and the idea that kindness is contagious. http://www.youtube.com/watch?v=5iC-xqyF6Us. There are many other video clips on this site about kindness.

The second resource is http://www.values.com. You will find inspirational stories, quotations, and a list of character traits which they believe make a difference in communities. In addition, they have podcasts, billboards, radio, and TV spots. The podcast below is 10:47 minutes in length. "No two softball players exemplify sportsmanship more than Mallory Holtman and Liz Wallace. These college athletes showed us that kindness and compassion are the real paths to victory when they carried their injured opponent around the bases after she hit a home run. http://www.values.com/inspirational-audio-stories/13-Sportsmanship. This is a touching and inspirational story.

Another Internet resource is Mr. Henry's Wild and Wacky World. You can join Mr. Henry as he uses scripture references, Bible stories, games, and puzzles to discover the truth about various character traits. You will learn surprising lessons about God and His word when you join the never ending action that fills Mr. Henry's workshop. These are longer presentations, but you can use them as a continuing story. It is a little wacky so be sure to preview the presentations before you use them. Have Fun!!! http://www.youtube.com/playlist?list=PL9A96710954DD6695

You may also choose to use **Kids of Integrity** http://www.kidsofintegrity.com/kindness. You will find Bible stories, texts, object lessons, and a variety of other tools which are free. As a faith-filled parent/teacher, you want to help your children develop Christ-like attitudes and behavior. But this important responsibility can seem overwhelming. How do you know where to start?

Kids of Integrity is a set of free resources that will help you coach your kids with confidence and a clear sense of direction. Better still, *Kids of Integrity* will excite your children about living "God's way."

Week Fourteen

Kindness

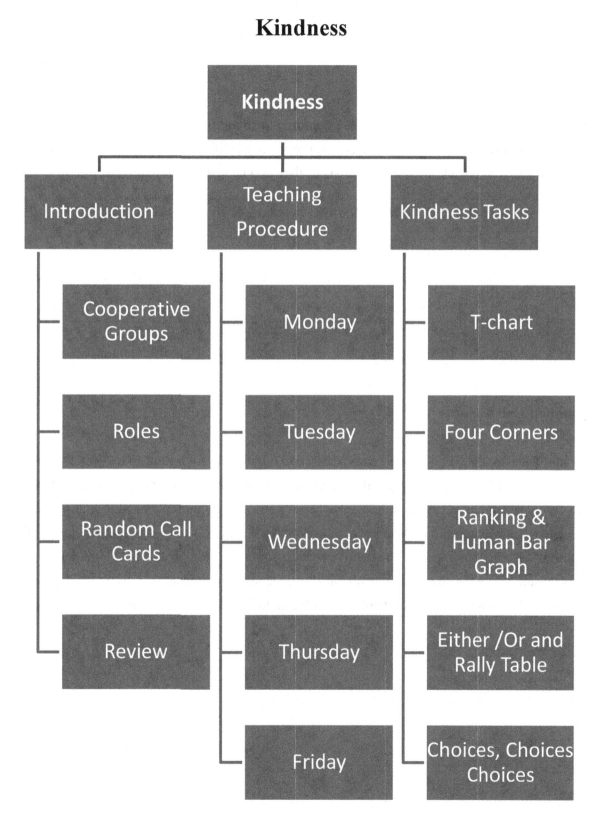

Cooperative Groups

Continue to reinforce the use of cooperative groups.

Roles

It is time to change roles. Remember, the persons in each group still keep the same number however now you change the roles. You continue to rotate through the roles each time you introduce a new character trait (see example below) or you may choose to change roles at the beginning of each week. Post the roles where they can be seen.

Week 11 & 12	Week 13 & 14	Week 15 & 16	Week 17 & 18
Reporter 3	Reporter 2	Reporter 1	Reporter 4
Recorder 4	Recorder 3	Recorder 2	Recorder 1
Materials Person 1	Materials Person 4	Materials Person 3	Materials Person 2
Social Skills/ Environment 2	Social Skills/ Environment 1	Social Skills/ Environment 4	Social Skills/ Environment 3

Random Call Cards

Continue to use the Random Call name cards and table cards for two primary purposes; one, for you to get better acquainted with the students, and second, as a means to call on them randomly when answers to questions or when reports on assignments need to be presented. As a teacher you need to always have your Random Call cards with you because randomly calling on participants is such an effective process for getting and keeping their attention. For this reason, you want to ensure that all cards are the same in appearance. Avoid using colors or marks that would help participants to discriminate their card from another.

Teaching Procedure Week Fourteen

Monday

T-Chart

"Now let's use a T-chart to find out what **kindness** '*looks like*' and '*sounds like.*'" (Draw a T-chart as illustrated on the next page on chart paper or on your computer screen). "What will a person say and do when they are **kind**? Remember, I am looking for concrete, observable behavior, something that you can hear someone say or see what they do." (Divide groups as needed, i.e., half of the classroom will complete *"looks like"* and the other half *"sounds like"* or 1's and 3's complete *"looks like"* and 2's and 4's will complete *"sounds like,"* etc.)

"I will give you 3 minutes to work in your groups. Try to think of 3 or 4 examples. Then I will call on the reporters to give me the responses . . . Time is up. I will use my Random Call cards to decide which table will share first. Then we will continue by using a Round Robin" (See Appendix.) "Allowing each group an opportunity to share one example." (Fill out the T-chart or invite a student who has good writing to fill it in as the teams share their suggestions.)

After completing one round (meaning that each group has had a chance to contribute), you may choose to do another round or you may open the floor for any suggestions which have not yet been recorded. When finished, post the T-chart in the classroom.

"We will post the T-chart where we all can see it. If we think of other examples of what perseverance '*looks like*' or '*sounds like*' during the week, we will add them to the T-chart."

T-Chart	

Kindness

Looks Like	Sounds Like

"Before we have prayer asking God to help us practice kindness, let's review the definition." You may have the entire class repeat it together, boys, then girls, different groups, etc. Remind them to practice obedience throughout the day and at home. Then finish with prayer.

Tuesday

Four Corners—You will need to write the name of 4 of the stories you read the last week on 8 1/2 by 11 sheets of paper. You may use white or colored paper.

Richard's Rubbish Heap	Kindness at Play or Orphan Arthur	The Day Oma Came Home	The Boy Who Said "Go On"

"Good morning class!!! It's time for worship. I would like you to use a Think-square-share to discuss how you were **kind** yesterday or if you noticed anyone else who was **kind**." (Give them from 30 seconds to 1 1/2 minutes to discuss.) "Now I will use my Random Call cards." (Call on 2-3 students and then open the floor.)

"Today we are going to use a Four Corners activity for our worship. You will notice the titles of 4 of the stories we read last week about kindness posted around the classroom, one on each wall. I want you to think of which story was your favorite story about **kindness**. Be sure to think of as many reasons for your choice as you can. Think individually. That's right; I should not hear any talking. Now that you have had time to think I want you to stand up and walk to the title you chose. Once everyone is standing by the title they chose, I want you to Turn-to-your-neighbor and talk about why you made the choice you did." (You will have to judge how much time they need, but do not give them too much time. Use the raising of your hand or whatever signal you use to get students' attention.)

"Now I will use Random Call cards. If I call your name then your group will begin (or you may begin with the corner that has the most people or least), and then we will continue around the classroom. We will use a Round Robin to call on each corner to give me one reason they heard or they presented . . . You have given some very good reasons. I will open the floor . . . Good work. You may go back to your seats."

Before prayer you may ask the following questions and have the entire class answer, or different groups, or individuals. "What's the word for this week? What is the definition? What is the text in the Bible that tells us we need to be **kind**? Excellent!!! You were able to tell me by memory what the definition of **kindness** is and the text in the Bible that tells us we need to **kind**. Let's bow our heads for prayer as we ask God to help us to continue to be kind."

Wednesday

Ranking—You will need to have a copy of the exercise so each student can access the information and work individually to complete the task of ranking three or more tasks in their order of preference or priority.

"This morning we are going to complete a ranking exercise for worship. I would like the materials person to come and take enough of the materials for each person in your group. Each of you needs to answer the question individually. Let's read the question together:

Which benefits you most? When others are:

_____ Pleasant/happy

_____ Generous/giving

_____ Considerate/understanding

_____ Friendly

"Remember this is about what you think: 1 = most important; 2 = next important; 3 = next; and 4 is least important. I am going to give you 3 minutes to work individually. After you have completed the task, you may discuss your ranking with your group.

"To complete this exercise let's create a Human Bar Graph. I have different pieces of paper on a wall/board with each paper having one of the choices written on it. Line up under your number one choice." (Students should be facing you so they form a bar graph. There are many connections you can help the students make at this time. Which has the most people? What can you learn from where people stood?) "Talk-to-your-neighbor and share why you made the choice you did for your number one choice. I will then call on some of you randomly. You can tell me what you said or what your neighbor said." Call on two or three and then open the floor to others who wish to respond.

"Excellent work!!! You were able to make a choice and explain why that choice was most important to you. You may return to your seat. Let's repeat the word, definition, and text before we have prayer today." Make any other observations that are appropriate to the lesson.

Thursday

Either/Or—You will need to write the words YOU/ OTHERS on 8 1/2 by 11 sheets of paper. You may use white or colored paper. Post these on opposite sides of the room.

"For worship today you will be able to participate in an Either/Or exercise. It is one of my favorites. It is like the Four Corners exercise we did on Monday, except that in an Either/Or exercise you only have two choices. Even though you may like both choices, you are forced to choose one and give your reasons for making that choice. Here is the question: Who benefits most from your kindness?

"Yes, you have to think first and I should hear no talking." (Give them time to think, perhaps 30 seconds). "Now you may go to the side of your choice. Turn-to-your-neighbor and talk about why you made the choice you did." You will have to judge how much time they need, but do not give them too much time. Use the raising of your hand or whatever signal you use to get students' attention.

"We will use a Rally Table to share your thoughts. Let's begin with those of you who chose others. Anyone in the group can give a reason they chose others or a reason someone else in the group chose others. Good, you were able to give a reason why you think others benefit most from your kindness. Now let's go to those who chose you. Give me just one reason. Let's go back to the other side. It is like playing tennis, you go back and forth." (Call on two or three and then open the floor to others who wish to respond. Share your choice at the end too).

"Well done. You were able to tell why you think you or others benefit most from your kindness. I appreciated hearing all the different ideas. You may go back to your seats." (Before prayer you could find out if they want to add anything else to the T-chart, make comments on those you have seen who have shown **kindness**, etc.)

Friday

Have each group illustrate **kindness**. Choices could include finding or creating:

1. Songs
   a. They can write their own words to a familiar tune or find a song
2. Find or create a story or speech
3. Skits/role play
4. Acronyms
5. Pictorials
6. Power Point presentation or other digital presentations
7. Videos they find or create or,
8. Combinations of these

"Remember, each person in the group has to be involved in the presentation. Have fun and make it memorable."

Special Note: Make this day special. Be creative!!!!!

Week Fifteen & Sixteen

Table of Contents

Week Fifteen

Patience

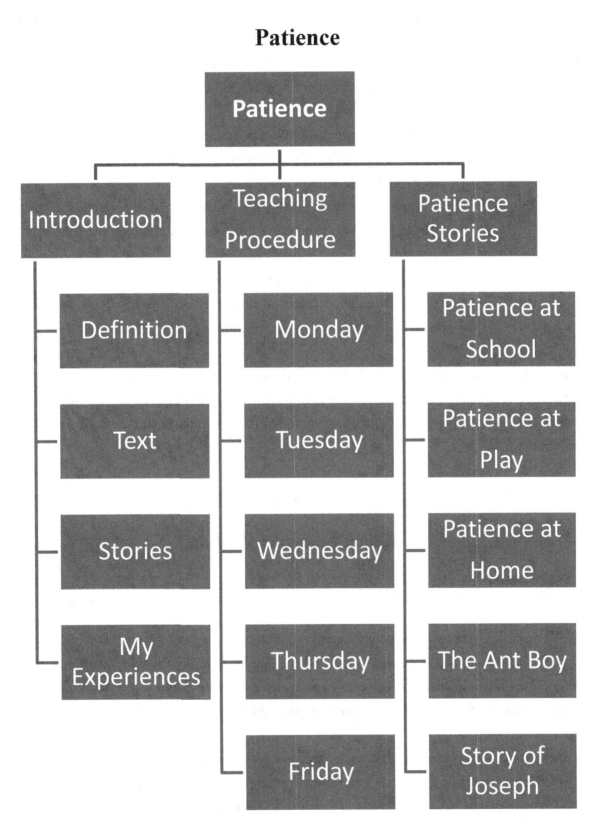

Patience

Definition:	Accepting a difficult situation without complaining. It also means waiting with a happy spirit.
Attributes:	(1) Ability to accept trouble or difficult situation, (2) You do not become angry or upset; (3) You do not complain; (4) You show a positive attitude
Text:	1 Thessalonians 5:14—"We ask you, brothers, to warn those who do not work. Encourage the people who are afraid. Help those who are weak. Be patient with every person."* ICB
Stories:	At the end of the week you may ask students to write about their favorite story/object lesson from those that were shared during the week.
My Experiences:	Students write about a personal experience involving the trait for the week. Students may take pictures and post, interview someone and post, prepare a short video, or other media enhanced method to present their experience.

You could also make a digital record of the word, definition, attributes, text, stories, and my experience and post it on the class webpage, wiki, or electronic notebook. However, it is imperative that you create a specific place for worship where students can see the information throughout the day.

* You may use another appropriate text if you choose.

Teaching Procedure Week 15

Monday

"Good morning. Turn-to-your-neighbor and tell them what the word is for this week. That's correct. The word is **patience.** Let's read together the meaning of the word **patience** using a complete sentence. **Patience** is accepting a difficult situation without complaining. It also means waiting with a happy spirit. That is hard to do sometimes, isn't it?

"For example, when I explain something new and you think you understand, but when you start working you can't remember, you raise your hand, but I'm working with someone else and there are people before you, what can you do to help you to be patient? Perhaps you can be efficient and start on something else while you wait. When you finish your lunch and can't wait to go out to play, you need to be patient until everyone is finished. You can see **patience** is a very important word.

"Is there a text in the Bible that tells us we need to have patience and develop this trait? Remember; use a complete sentence in your answer. Let's reply together. The text in the Bible that tells us to be patient is 1 Thessalonians5:14—'We ask you, brothers, to warn those who do not work. Encourage the people who are afraid. Help those who are weak. Be patient with every person.'"

Talk about the weekend or read the story "Patience at School." (p. 204)

Pray—"When we pray, let's ask God to help us develop **patience**."

Tuesday

"Good morning, class! I appreciate how efficient all of you have been this morning. Everyone is ready for worship, and I can see students who are ready to listen with their ears, eyes, and heart. Fantastic! Use a complete sentence to tell your neighbor the word we are studying this week." (Reply—"The word we are studying this week is **patience.**") "Well done. Now use a complete sentence to repeat the definition of **patience** to a different neighbor at your table.

"I'm going to give you two minutes to learn the definition." (Wait two minutes.) "Turn-to-your-neighbor and repeat the definition." (Reply—"**Patience** is accepting a difficult situation without complaining. It also means waiting with a happy spirit." Make sure everyone has a turn and praise them. Remember to be specific with your praise.

"All of you did such a good job of repeating the definition word-for-word. Let's all say it together." (Reply—"The word we are studying this week is **patience. Patience** is accepting a difficult situation without complaining. It also means waiting with a happy spirit.")

Read: "Patience at Play" story. (p. 205)

"Next we will use the Think-square-share structure. Think individually about the answers to the questions about the story." (Give students time to think and then continue). "You may now square with your group and discuss your responses. The recorder will write and the reporter will report. Social skills persons, make sure all are involved in squaring."

Ask Questions: Use Think-pair-share. Use Random Call cards to share.

1. Why was it hard to be **patient** in this story? (Comprehension, Interpretive)
2. Who was having a hard time waiting? (Literal, Knowledge)
3. Do you think she was happy that she had been **patient**? Why? (Critical, Evaluation)
4. How can you be **patient** in the classroom, at home? At recess? (Application, Synthesis, Creative)

Call on different groups (tables, perhaps two) to report—they can each give one example and then open the floor.

"Your assignment is to observe when your classmates or you are practicing **patience**. We will talk about it again tomorrow."

Challenge students: "I want you to go out of your way to be patient not only at school, but also at home. Then, during the week we will share how we have been patient. This is a trait I'm going to work on really hard too."

Pray: "Let's ask God to help us develop this important character trait."

Wednesday

"Good morning, class. This morning let's try to repeat the word and the definition of the word we have been studying without looking at the board. Let's try it. Remember, we must use a complete sentence." (Reply—"The word we are studying this week is **patience**, and the definition of the word **patience** is accepting a difficult situation without complaining. It also means waiting with a happy spirit.") "Very good. This morning I was able to put this character trait into practice. There was a traffic jam and I was getting ready to complain when I remembered our word. Instead, I sang one of my favorite songs and felt much better for doing it. Did anyone practice patience yesterday or this morning? Turn-to-your-neighbor and tell them about it. I will use my Random Call cards to have you share with the class." Let two or three people share and then open the floor.

"Today, I'm going to give you three minutes to learn the verse. Remember you must use a complete sentence." You'll need to say, "The text in the Bible that helps us to be **patient** is 1 Thessalonians5:14—'We ask you, brothers, to warn those who do not work. Encourage the people who are afraid. Help those who are weak. Be patient with every person.'

"Practice in your head for 1minute. Then use a Round Robin or Turn-to-your-neighbor and continue to practice the verse. I will tell you when you can begin to practice with others. Ready, Start." After one minute, give them the signal to practice with others if they wish.

"Who is ready? I see many hands." Randomly call on one student. Let everyone try and give them all positive reinforcement. Remember the praise needs to be specific. For example, "Bill, you were willing and able to say the verse first and without any errors. Good work."

Read: "Patience at Home" story (p.206).

Ask Questions:

Use Think-pair-share. Use Random Call cards to share.

1. Who was **patient** in the story? (Literal, Knowledge)
2. In what ways was he/she/they **patient**? (Comprehension)
3. Can you think of an example of someone who was patient in the Bible? (Application)
4. In what area do you need to develop **patience**? (Synthesis, Critical)

Pray: "Thank God for giving us examples to follow."

Teacher: During the day, always comment on those who are practicing **patience**.

Thursday

"Good morning, class! Everyone is being so efficient. Excellent. Today is the day we say the word, the definition, and the text using a complete sentence without looking at the board.

"I'll give you four minutes to review the word, definition, and text." (Change the amount of time as needed.) "I will be practicing too. Remember you must use a complete sentence.

201

Let's read it together first. The word we are studying this week is **patience. Patience** is accepting a difficult situation without complaining. It means waiting with a happy spirit. The text in the Bible that tells us to be patient is 1 Thessalonians5:14—'We ask you, brothers, to warn those who do not work. Encourage the people who are afraid. Help those who are weak. Be patient with every person.'

"Let me try." (Go ahead and say it.) "Turn-to-your-neighbor and repeat the word, definition, and text we are leaning this week. Let's all say it together without looking. Good job!!!"

Read: "The Ant Boy" story. (p.207).

Answer Questions: Use a Think-square-share and Random Call cards to answer the following questions:

1. Who was **patient** in this story? (Literal, Knowledge)
2. How was the person **patient**? (Comprehension)
3. How can **patience** help you be a better student? (Application, Creative, Synthesis)
4. Who has noticed a classmate who has been **patient**? Be sure to include in what ways they were **patient**. (Application, Analysis)

Pray: "Let's ask God to help us develop patience."

Friday

"Good morning, class!" (Remember, this is a special day!)

How to Make It a Special Day

1. Invite a visitor, the pastor, or another teacher to make a presentation.
2. Let students sit with a friend as they finish the notebook page or border page.
3. Begin telling the story of Joseph then discuss how he had to be patient. Be Dramatic, and as soon as you signal for worship and they are ready, start with, "No, no. It's not fair. Please, I want to go home, etc." Make the story come alive!!!
4. Supply students with magazines and ask them to make up a story or to use the experience from the week to tell a story with pictures. It would be good if you had an example of your experience to show them.
5. Show the story of Joseph on DVD. It is available from Adventist Book Center or other Christian stores.

Repeat the word, definition, and text all together first. Remember to have anyone who did not say it the day before, say it today.

"Today all of you need to show me where you have written the word, text, definition, stories, and your experience on paper just as I have it on board. Under stories, write one of the stories you remember that we discussed this week, telling how the person was **patient**" (Knowledge, Comprehension). "Under experience, write what you did to be **patient** here or at home" (Application). "You may also write the definition and text on another piece of paper and decorate it" (Knowledge, Creativity). "You could give this to one of your parents or another teacher. Who else might enjoy these?" (Family members, shut-ins, teachers, and the pastor may enjoy them.)

Students may begin writing these as early as Monday but save the decorating of the paper for Friday. You just want them to make a notebook or portfolio. These may be either paper or ink or electronic. Be sure they keep a list of the words so they can review them later.

Special Note: Make this day special. Be creative!!!!!

Pray: "Ask God to help us to remember the good traits we've learned."

Stories of Patience

Patience at School

Patty burst into the classroom. "He's bleeding, he's bleeding!" she shouted.

Startled, Mrs. Kelly jumped up from her desk and hurried into the hall. A crowd of children was standing around the drinking fountain.

"Please stand back, children. Let me have some room," she said firmly.

As the children parted, she saw Robbie, in the center, holding his mouth. Blood was trickling down between his fingers and onto the floor.

"What happened?" asked Mrs. Kelly.

"Well," said Patty, all out of breath, "We were all waiting in line for a drink. Someone at the end of the line pushed, and we all bumped into one another, Robbie was drinking and hit his tooth on the drinking fountain."

Gently wiping away the blood, Mrs. Kelly opened Robbie's mouth to see how badly his lip was cut. She carefully applied a cold towel to his lip, to prevent any swelling.

"You will be fine, Robbie," she said calmly. "There is only a small cut on your lip. Your tooth looks all right."

The children all looked at the floor when she turned to them. "We are very fortunate," she said, "that Robbie was not injured more seriously. Not being patient can cause someone to get injured. Let's remember this lesson, so that no one ever gets hurt at the drinking fountain again."

From *A Child's Book of Character Building—Book 1*
by permission of Association of Christian Schools International

Patience at Play

"I wonder if the paint is dry enough," thought Patty. "Mother said to wait until after supper."

Circling the freshly painted swing set, she was careful not to let her dress touch the metal. How it glistened in the sun, with its shining new coat of red paint!

Maybe, if I just touch it with one finger, she said to herself, then I would know if it is still wet.

Cautiously, she reached out her finger. Then quickly, she pulled it back.

Mother said this paint only comes off with smelly paint remover. I would hate to have to wash my hands with that, thought Patty.

Again, she walked around the swing, studying it closely. I could touch it with a piece of paper, she reasoned. It no red paint came off, I would know that it was dry.

Patty quickly found a stick and wrapped some old newspaper on it. Before she tried it, she changed her mind.

If the paper is still wet, the paper will stick to it and leave a mark, Patty remembered.

So, with a sigh, she decided to wait until after supper. As she was helping with the dishes, her mother said, "Patty, I know it has been hard to wait with a happy spirit for the paint to dry. Because you have been so patient, you may have some ice cream when you have finished swinging."

From *A Child's Book of Character Building—Book 1*
by permission of Association of Christian Schools International

Patience at Home

"Mother's spaghetti!" shrieked Patty. "It's my favorite!"

Her mother smiled. "I knew you would be happy. Your father has worked very hard today, fixing the car. He is going to enjoy it, too."

Quickly, Patty ran in the backyard, she called her two younger sisters and hurriedly helped them to wash for dinner. Then they helped set the table and sat down.

"Why are we waiting?" questioned Patty.

"Well," responded Mother, "I called your father just a minute ago. He said he was coming. Let's be polite and wait patiently until everyone gets to the table."

Patty folded her hands in her lap, and so did her sister. Mother kept working in the kitchen to prepare the last few details of the meal.

Watching the steam rise from the spaghetti, Patty thought, "I wish Father would hurry. Spaghetti is only good when it is hot."

Moments passed that seemed liked hours. Her sisters began to wiggle.

Anxiously, they asked, "May we eat now, Mother?"

"No, not until Father gets here," she said. "He will be finished soon. Please wait with happy spirits."

Just then, Father walked in with a big smile on his greasy face. "Thank you, girls," he said, "for being so patient."

From *A Child's Book of Character Building—Book 1*
by permission of Association of Christian Schools International

The Ant Boy

Auguste Forel was 11 years old. Just like all the other boys in his neighborhood, he went to school every morning and came home every afternoon. But when the other boys met in the park to play baseball, he wasn't always with them. Usually he was in his own backyard, squatting down and watching something on the ground very closely.

Auguste studied ants. Hundreds and hundreds of ants lived in his backyard, and he was fascinated in watching them crawl in almost a straight line from one hole to the other. Then, one by one, they would disappear into the hole.

He wondered what they did in those holes. Carefully he scraped away of the dirt. And there, deep in the dirt, he found the ant's hallways and round rooms. Some had rotted leaves and dead ants, others were filled with motionless ants in white cocoons. They looked sort of like babies in blankets. Auguste notices that as soon as he scrapes away the dirt, special ants called "nurse ants" hurried to those in the cocoons and carried them away, one by one from danger.

Day after day he patiently studied the ants. He discovered that there were big ants and little ones, ants with wings, and black, red and yellow ants. Each ant had a job to do, and they seemed to do their work without any rest.

One day when Auguste was pretty familiar with his ants, he noticed that inside the nests of the big black ants were tiny passageways that belonged to little red ants. The little red ants were sneaky, they used their tiny size to get what they needed.

The little red ants would slip into the big black ants' tunnels and snatch away some of the food that the larger ants were storing away. When the big ants would try to stop the tiny red ants, the tiny ones would get together and bite the big ants so hard that they would soon flee. Then the red ants would run with the food into their tiny passageways, where the big ants couldn't follow.

It made Auguste think that even though he was just a little boy—just as the ants were little—he could do things that the big people couldn't. He had time to study ants, but the big people didn't. So everything he saw, Auguste wrote down in a book. And when he was older, people listened to what "the Ant Man" had learned about insects. He soon became

207

famous. Remember, he was only eleven, and he was just studying ants in his backyard when he started, but he had patience and did the very best he could do, and that's how he learned things that even grown-up scientists didn't know. You see good things happen when we (are patient and) do the very best we can?

From Daily Devotional *Out of This World*
by permission of Nancy Beck Irland

More Resources on Patience

The resources below may be used during the second week if you would like to include a story on a particular day. You may also choose to use some of these stories if you are only dealing with upper graders during the first week.

The first resource is **Kids of Integrity** http://www.kidsofintegrity.com/patience. You will find Bible stories, texts, object lessons, and a variety of other tools which are free. They have several object lessons you may enjoy using for patience.

As a faith-filled parent/teacher, you want to help your children develop Christ-like attitudes and behavior. But this important responsibility can seem overwhelming. How do you know where to start?

Kids of Integrity is a set of free resources that will help you coach your kids with confidence and a clear sense of direction. Better still, *Kids of Integrity* will excite your children about living "God's way."

The second resource is http://www.values.com. You will find inspirational stories, quotations, and a list of character traits which they believe make a difference in communities. In addition, they have podcasts, billboards, radio and TV spots. The two TV spots below are very short but they make the point. Patience is hardest to find when you need it the most! In this charming moment where a young boy innocently sloshes through wet cement we find ourselves asking the question, "What would I do?" just as we find out. We think your will smile with relief and take away a good reminder. http://www.values.com/inspirational-stories-tv-spots/107-Wet-Cement

Patience . . . Pass it on (30 seconds).

Based on a true story, this poignant moment in a concert hall reminds us how even the most embarrassing situations can be turned around with a little patience and encouragement. http://www.values.com/inspirational-stories-tv-spots/100-Concert (60 seconds).

The third resource is from www.youtube.com. The two video clips below are the same. The longer one is very good, but does have a spelling error. They talk about growing bamboo and the patience it takes to grow it. http://www.youtube.com/watch?v=bo8siqfciHo&feature=related (2:10 in length) http://www.youtube.com/watch?v=KquifznJX_4 (4:09 in length)

Week Sixteen

Patience

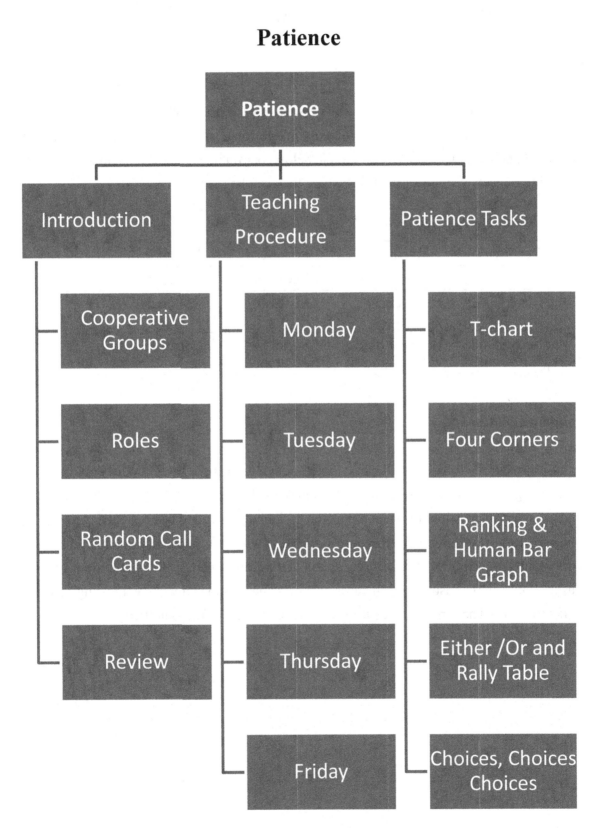

Cooperative Groups

Continue to reinforce the use of cooperative groups.

Roles

It is time to change roles. Remember, the persons in each group still keep the same number however now you change the roles. You continue to rotate through the roles each time you introduce a new character trait (see example below) or you may choose to change roles at the beginning of each week. Post the roles where they can be seen.

Week 11 & 12	Week 13 & 14	Week 15 & 16	Week 17 & 18
Reporter 3	Reporter 2	Reporter 1	Reporter 4
Recorder 4	Recorder 3	Recorder 2	Recorder 1
Materials Person 1	Materials Person 4	Materials Person 3	Materials Person 2
Social Skills/ Environment 2	Social Skills/ Environment 1	Social Skills/ Environment 4	Social Skills/ Environment 3

Random Call Cards

Continue to use the Random Call name cards and table cards for two primary purposes; one, for you to get better acquainted with them, and second, as a means to call on them randomly when answers to questions or when reports on assignments need to be presented. As a teacher you need to always have your Random Call cards with you because randomly calling on participants is such an effective process for getting and keeping their attention. For this reason, you want to ensure that all cards are the same in appearance. Avoid using colors or marks that would help participants to discriminate their card from another.

Teaching Procedure Week 16

Monday

T-Chart

"Now let's use a T-chart to find out what **patience** '*looks like*' and '*sounds like.*'" (Draw a T-chart as illustrated on the next page on chart paper or on your computer screen). "What will a person say and do when they are **patient**? Remember, I am looking for concrete, observable behavior, something that you can hear someone say or see what they do." (Divide groups as needed, i.e., half of the classroom will complete "*looks like*" and the other half "*sounds like*" or 1's and 3's complete "*looks like*" and 2's and 4's will complete "*sounds like,*" etc.)

"I will give you 3 minutes to work in your groups. Try to think of 3 or 4 examples. Then I will call on the reporters to give me the responses . . . Time is up. I will use my Random Call cards to decide which table will share first. Then we will continue by using a Round Robin" (See Appendix.) "Allowing each group an opportunity to share one example." Fill out the T-chart or invite a student who has good writing to fill it in as the teams share their suggestions.

After completing one round, (meaning that each group has had a chance to contribute), you may choose to do another round or you may open the floor for any suggestions which have not yet been recorded. When finished, post the T-chart in the classroom.

"We will post the T-chart where we all can see it. If we think of other examples of what perseverance '*looks like*' or '*sounds like*' during the week, we will add them to the T-chart."

T-Chart	

Patience

Looks Like	Sounds Like

"Before we have prayer asking God to help us practice **patience**, let's review the definition." You may have the entire class repeat it together, boys, then girls, different groups, etc. Remind them to practice obedience throughout the day and at home. Then finish with prayer.

Tuesday

Four Corners—You will need to write the name of 4 of the stories you read about patience on 81/2 by 11 sheets of paper. You may use white or colored paper.

Patience at School	Patience at Play	Patience at Home	The Ant Boy

"Good morning class!!! It's time for worship. I would like you to use a Think-square-share to discuss how you were **patient** yesterday or if you noticed anyone else who was **patient.**" (Give them from 30 seconds to 1 1/2 minutes to discuss). "Now I will use my Random Call cards." Call on 2-3 students and then open the floor.

"Today we are going to use a Four Corners activity for our worship. You will notice the titles of 4 of the stories we read last week about **patience** posted around the classroom, one on each wall. I want you to think of which story was your favorite story about **patience**. Be sure to think of as many reasons for your choice as you can. Think individually. That's right; I should not hear any talking. Now that you have had time to think I want you to stand up and walk to the title you chose. Once everyone is standing by the title they chose, I want you to Turn-to-your-neighbor and talk about why you made the choice you did." You will have to judge how much time they need, but do not give them too much time. Use the raising of your hand or whatever signal you use to get students' attention.

"Now I will use Random Call cards. If I call your name then your group will begin (or you may begin with the corner that has the most people or least), and then we will continue around the classroom. We will use a Round Robin to call on each corner to give me one reason they heard or they presented . . . You have given some very good reasons. I will open the floor . . . Good work. You may go back to your seats."

Before prayer you may ask the following questions and have the entire class answer, or different groups, or individuals. "What's the word for this week? What is the definition? What is the text in the Bible that tells us we need to be **patient**? Excellent!! You were able to tell me word-for-word what the definition of **patience** is and the text in the Bible that tells us we need to **patient**. Let's bow our heads for prayer as we ask God to help us to continue to be patient."

Wednesday

Ranking—You will need to have a copy of the exercise so each student can access the information and work individually to complete the task of ranking three or more tasks in their order of preference or priority.

"This morning we are going to complete a ranking exercise for worship. I would like the materials person to come and take enough of the materials for each person in your group. Each of you needs to answer the question individually. Let's read the question together:

Which do you think are the best examples of patience?

_____ Being pleasant about cleaning around other's desks even though it is recess time

_____ Happily allowing a younger child to get in lunch line ahead of you

_____ Being pleasant about helping someone solve a problem even though they want to give up

_____ Being happy about helping others to complete their task before you are finished with yours

"Remember this is about what you think: 1 = most important; 2 = next important; 3 = next; and 4 is least important. I am going to give you 2 minutes to work individually. After you have completed the task, you may discuss your ranking with your group.

"To complete this exercise let's create a Human Bar Graph. I have four different pieces of paper on a wall/board with each paper having one of the choices written on it. Line up under your number one choice." (Students should be facing you so they form a bar graph. There are many connections you can help the students make at this time. Which has the most people? What can you learn from where people stood?) "Talk-to-your-neighbor and share why you made the choice you did for your number one. I will then call on some of you randomly. You can tell me what you said or what your neighbor said." Call on two or three and then open the floor to others who wish to respond.

"Excellent work!!! You were able to make a choice and explain why that choice was most important to you. You may return to your seat. Let's repeat the word, definition, and text before we have prayer today." Make any other observations that are appropriate to the lesson.

Thursday

Either/Or—You will need to write the words YES/ NO on 8 1/2 by 11 sheets of paper. You may use white or colored paper. Post these on opposite sides of the room.

YES	NO

"For worship today you will be able to participate in an Either/Or exercise. Remember, even though you may like both choices, you are forced to choose one and give your reasons for making that choice. Here is the question: Would people who know me well describe me as a patient person?

"Yes, you have to think first and I should hear no talking" (Give them time to think, perhaps 30 seconds). "Now you may go to the side of your choice. Turn-to-your-neighbor and talk about why you made the choice you did." You will have to judge how much time they need, but do not give them too much time. Use the raising of your hand or whatever signal you use to get students' attention.

"We will use a Rally Table to share your thoughts. In a Rally Table one person from one side gives a reason then another person from the other side shares a reason. Let's begin with those of you who chose yes. Anyone in the group can give a reason they chose yes or a reason someone else in the group chose yes. Good, you were able to give a reason why people think you are a patient person. Now let's go to those who chose no. Give me just one reason. Let's go back to the other side. It is like playing tennis, you go back and forth." Call on two or three and then open the floor to others who wish to respond. Share your choice at the end too.

"Well done. You were able to tell why you think people would describe you as a patient person. I appreciated hearing all the different ideas. You may go back to your seats." (Before prayer you could find out if they want to add anything else to the T-chart, make comments on those you have seen who have shown perseverance, etc.)

Friday

Have each group illustrate **patience**. Choices could include finding or creating:

1. Songs
   a. They can write their own words to a familiar tune or find a song
2. Find or create a story or speech
3. Skits/role play
4. Acronyms
5. Pictorials
6. Power Point presentation or other digital presentations
7. Videos they find or create or,
8. Combinations of these

Remember, each person in the group has to be involved in the presentation. Have fun and make it memorable.

Special Note: Make this day special. Be creative!!!!!

Week Seventeen

Table of Contents

Week Seventeen

Culminating Activities

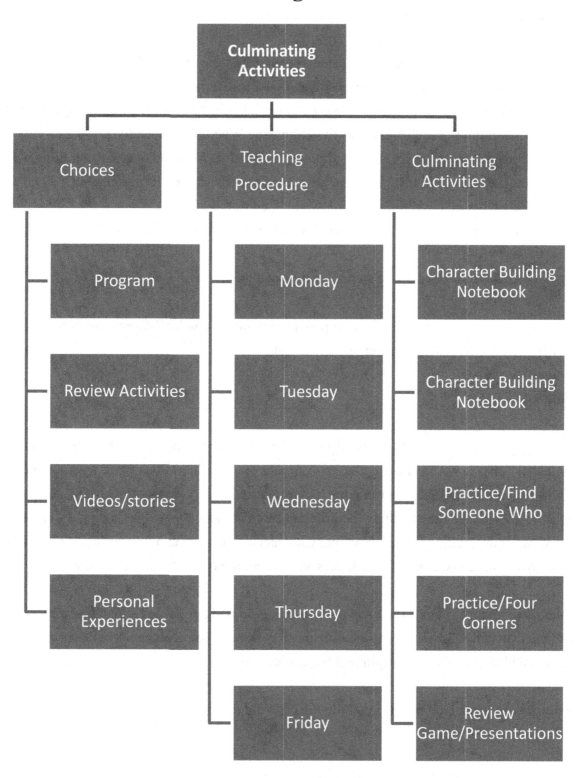

Teaching Procedure Culminating Activities

This week is to be used as a review week. There are so many activities that you may use one or two weeks for review. Depending on your facilities, you may choose several activities to do. The following are only suggestions:

1. Show a video story that may last all week. Each time discuss character traits.
2. Let students listen to a "Story Hour" CD while they finish notebooks.
3. Review by using (a) Family Feud as in week six, (b) Numbered Heads Together, (c) Classroom Baseball and or (d) Find Someone Who (See Appendix.)
4. Practice for a program Sabbath morning. Have students write the character traits with the definition and text on border sheets to give out after their presentation.
5. Play Character-Building Countdown on the last day.
6. Review two character traits each day. Have students repeat the word, definition and text.
7. Discuss how developing the trait has helped them.

Use the questions from Family Feud to play classroom baseball. Different questions will be worth a run to first base or second or a home run.

Monday

"Good morning. Today during worship time, I want to see everyone's Character Building Notebook. If it is not neat or if you want to add stories, this is the week to complete it. I will let you sit with a friend as long as you are quiet. If you are already finished with your notebook, take time to study the different traits because we will be having a Character Building Countdown! Let's see how many character traits you can use during this worship time. Will you be obedient, efficient, persevering, attentive . . . ? I'll be checking.

"Our worship time is over. The notebooks are really looking good. Let's go back to our seats and then we will have prayer. I want to thank all of you for being obedient." (Be specific and find something specific to compliment the children for.)

Pray: "Let's thank God for the good job the class did during worship."

Tuesday

"Good morning. If you have not finished your notebook, you may work on it today. Those who are finished may listen to a story. Then we will find out what character traits were in the story."

Play a CD, or use a story, video clip or other activity from the More Resources sections.

Ask Questions: Use a Think-square-share or a Turn-to-your-neighbor and Random Call cards.

1. What character traits did you notice? (Literal, Knowledge)
2. How did the person demonstrate that trait? (Comprehension)
3. What is your favorite trait that we have studied? Why? (Analysis, Evaluation)

Pray: "Let's ask God to also help us develop" [name the trait(s)] "identified from the story."

Teacher: If you are planning to present the Sabbath School or church program, give out the parts to the students and have each student practice his or her part. If you have a small class, each student can recite the word, definition, and the text. If you have a larger class, one student could say the word, one the definition, and one the text. Take advantage of this opportunity to teach the students how to speak in public. They need to speak clearly, stand straight, look at the audience, etc.

Wednesday

Teacher: Today, if you are practicing for a program, emphasize the use of all the character traits during practice time. Are they listening for your directions? Are they doing willingly what they are told to do? Are they being kind? etc.

If you are not planning a program, today you can use the People Hunt/ Find Someone Who activity as a review. It is found in the Appendix. If you have more time students can continue to quiz each other in readiness for the countdown the next day. Of course, they must all work on their notebooks if not completed.

Take time to walk around the classroom and compliment students on their work. Catch them doing something good!!!

Pray: "Let's ask God to help us not only to say these traits but to put them into practice."

Thursday

Four Corners—You will need to write the name of the 4 of the structures you have used on 8 1/2 by 11 sheets of paper. You may use white or colored paper.

T-Chart	Four Corners	Ranking	Either/Or

"Today we are going to use a Four Corners activity for our worship. You will notice the names of four (4) of the structures we used during worship time posted around the classroom, one on each wall. I want you to think of which structure is your favorite. Be sure to think of as many reasons for your choice as you can. Think individually. That's right; I should not hear any talking . . . Now that you have had time to think I want you to stand up and walk to the structure you chose. Once everyone is standing at the corner of their choice, I want you to Turn-to-your-neighbor and talk about why you made the choice you did." You will have to judge how much time they need, but do not give them too much time. Use the raising of your hand or whatever signal you use to get students' attention.

"Now I will use Random Call cards. If I call your name then your group will begin" (or you may begin with the corner that has the most people or least), "and then we will continue around the classroom. We will use a Round Robin to call on each corner to give me one reason they heard or they presented." (Continue for 2 turns.) "You have given some very good reasons. I will open the floor . . . Good work. You may go back to your seats."

Pray: "Thank God for the many different ways we learn."

Friday

Character-Building Countdown

"Today we will find out how many of you can remember the traits. I want everyone to stand and line up against the wall. I'll ask you a question. If you answer it correctly, you may go to the front of the line. If you miss the question, you must go to the end of the line. Here we go:

Suggested Questions:

1. Recite Matthew 19:23.
2. Name a story that shows perseverance in the Bible.
3. Give the definition for efficiency.
4. What are these words that we are studying called?
5. Which character trait is one of my favorites?
6. Give the text and recite the verse that tells us to be obedient.
7. What word means to continue to do something in spite of difficulties or obstacles?
8. When Gideon chose men to fight for him, he chose men that were what?
9. Give the text that tells us to listen.
10. What is another word for listen?
11. Recite the text that tells us to be efficient.
12. Tell one way you were efficient at home.
13. In which definition does the word willingly appear?
14. Recite James 1:19.
15. Recite Ecclesiastes 9:10.
16. What is the only thing that we can take to heaven?
17. Mention a story that shows the importance of being efficient.
18. Define attentiveness.
19. Define obedience.
20. Give the first six words in order that we studied them.
21. What is character?
22. Define honesty.
23. What character trait does Proverbs 20:11 tell us about?
24. Recite Philippians 4:8.
25. What will help your reputation?

26. Define patience.

27. Repeat Ephesians 4:32.

28. Which text in the Bible tells us we need to develop patience?

29. What character trait does a pleasant, friendly action describe?

30. Tell us how you have been patient.

You may change, add, or subtract as many questions as you wish.

Remember, Teacher:

A student's life is a book
with pages all empty and clean;
for whom One died and then arose,
Fulfilling God's Master Plan.

Oh! How great the responsibility,
For souls in the balance stand;

but we can all make the
DIFFERENCE
Building by the Master's Plan.

Anonymous
God bless you . . .

Appendix

Table of Contents

In this section of the appendix, we list basic teaching structures suggested for use in the book. Each structure is listed with a step-by-step process outline designed to enable you to easily translate the process into your teaching repertoire. Each structure is designed to enable you, the teacher, to get all of your students to respond to planned questions and activities. This is important because it is difficult to influence someone if we do not know what they are thinking. When students respond to you, you have a much more likely chance to influence their thinking. That is, after all, our primary job. Secondly, there is information included in the appendix in regard to asking questions. A step-by-step process is suggested that will enable you to get all of your students to reply all of the time.

Response Structures

Random Call
Step-by-Step

Before beginning instruction, the teacher writes each student's name on a 3x5 file card. The teacher could choose to have each student write his/her own name on a card.

Step 1. Teacher asks a question
Step 2. Students think
Step 3. You can increase the interaction level of Random Call by having students **Turn-To-Your-Neighbor, Pair** or **Square** before moving to step four.
Step 4. Teacher draws a card
Step 5. Teacher calls on that student
Step 6. Student responds
Step 7. Return the card to the deck

Corners
Step-by-Step

Corners is a cooperative structure that requires students to choose from four different options and then verbalize the reasons for their choice. Here is the procedure for corners:

Step 1. Present the question and possible answers
Step 2. Think time

        a.   Students decide on their personal choice

Step 3.   Announce corners

        a.   You can actually post the choices in the different corners

Step 4.   Students move to corners

        a.   Form pairs and justify reasons for their choice

Step 5.   *Paraphrase

        a.   Pairs form groups and paraphrase their partner's response

Step 6.   Corners report

        a.   Teacher calls on students from one corner to announce to the class reasons for their choice

Step 7.   *Corners paraphrase

        a.   Student pairs in the other corners paraphrase these reasons. Step 6 and Step 7 are repeated for each corner.

Step 8.   *Teams review

        a.   Make sure everyone in each team can name reasons for supporting each choice.

* There steps are optional.

Ranking Exercise
Step-by-Step

Ranking is a response structure that requires students to rearrange in their order of preferences or priority three or more different options and then verbalize the reasons for their priority. Here is the procedure for doing a ranking exercise.

Step 1.   Present the question or statement with three or more different responses

Step 2.   Students rank or prioritize the different responses

        a.   Students consider different options and make their personal choice.

Step 3.   Students explain and defend their responses

        a.   Students form pairs and express reasons for their choices

Step 4.   Students share with home group

        a.   Pairs discuss their priorities and reasons

Step 5.   Students share with the class

        a.   This can be done in a variety of ways:

                i.   Form a Human Bar Graph

ii.   Use Corners

iii. Call on the reporter

iv.   Call on individuals (Random Call cards)

Sample Ranking Exercise

Which of the following would help you most in learning the meaning of faith? (1=most important; 2=next most important: etc.)

_____ Exploring the way the Bible defines faith?

_____ Listening to a theologian talk on faith

_____ Putting yourself in Jesus' hands in a risky situation

_____ Listening to experiences of others who have lived in faith

Source: *Project Affirmation: Teaching Values* (1996) by Roland and Doris Larson with Bailey Gillespie, Riverside, CA: La Sierra University Press. Available through your college bookstore or the local Adventist Book Center.

Either/Or
Step-by-Step

Either/or is a response structure. It is a forced choice between two options that requires students to select the option with which they most closely identify. Here is the procedure for doing an either/or exercise.

Step 1. Teacher poses a question with two alternatives

Step 2. Think time

a. Students decide on their personal choice

Step 3. Teacher points to opposite sides of the room and identifies the alternatives

a. You can post the alternatives on the opposite sides of the room

Step 4. Students move to opposite sides

Step 5. Students Turn-to-a-Neighbor

a. Students Turn-to-a-neighbor and shares the reason(s) for their choices

Step 6. Students share with the whole class

a. Students may share their own idea or that of their partner. There are many structures to accomplish this. You decide which to use:

i. **Random Call**—Have students' names on 3x5 cards and randomly draw names and call on the students.

ii. **Volunteers**—Be careful or the same students will respond every time.

iii. **Rally Table**—One person from one side gives a reason and then one person from the other side shares a reason. This continues until you stop the process.

Turn-to-your-neighbor and Share

Step-by-Step

Step 1. Teacher poses a question

Step 2. Individuals *think* about their answer

a. You may request the students to write down their ideas.

Step 3. Students form *pairs*

a. Students discuss their ideas with a partner. The simplest way to form pairs is to have the students turn to the person sitting next to them. Or if students are sitting in groups of four, have the foursome form two pairs. You may end up with one group of three since many classes have an odd number of students.

Step 4. Students *share* with the whole class

a. Students may share their own idea or that of their partner. There are many techniques to accomplish this. You decide which to use:

1. **Random Call**—Have students' names on 3x5 cards and randomly draw names and to call on students. o**r**

2 **Volunteers**—Be careful or the same students will respond every time.

Think-Pair-Square

Step-by-Step

Step 1. Teacher poses a question

Step 2. Individuals **think** about their answer

    a. You may request the students to write down their ideas.

Step 3. Students form **pairs**

    a. Students discuss their ideas with a partner from their team. Have teams of four form two pairs. Teams with five members will result in one group of three. This is not unusual since many classes have an odd number of students.

Step 4. Students **square** with their cooperative group (**square** assumes that groups have been formed with four members in each group)

    a. Students discuss their ideas/responses with their full team. They may share their own idea of that of their partner from step 3.

Think-Square-Share

Step-by-Step

Step 1. Teacher poses a question

Step 2. Individuals **think** about their answer

    a. You may request the students to write down their ideas.

Step 3. Students **square** with their cooperative group (**square** assumes that groups have been formed with four members in each group)

    a. All team members discuss their ideas with each other.

Step 4. Students **share** with the whole class

    a. Students may share their own idea or that of a team member. Use Random Call cards for this purpose.

Rally Table

Step 1. Teacher poses a question

Step 2. Individuals **think** about their answers

Step 3. Students form pairs

    a. Students discuss their ideas with a partner from their team. Have teams of four form two pairs. Teams with five members will result in one group of three. This is not unusual since many classes have an odd number of students.

Step 4. Pairs alternatingly report to each other

    a. Pair one gives an answer, then pair two gives an answer, pair one gives an additional point, then pair two gives an additional point until all answers are given or the teacher calls time.

Step 5. Students share with the whole class

    a. Use Random Call cards for this purpose.

Round Table

Step-by-Step

Step 1. Teacher poses a question

Step 2. First student writes

    a. The first student in each group writes down a response and passes the paper to the second student

Step 3. Second student writes

    a. The second student writes down a response and passes the paper to the next student

Step 4. Process continues around the table

    a. This process is completed with no talking.

Notes:

1. For some questions, you may want the group to send the paper around the table only once. For other questions you may want to have the paper go around the table several times, sort of like a silent brainstorm session.

2. Typically, after the paper has gone around the table the teacher has plans for discussing/ sharing individual team responses with at least one other team or even the whole class. It is common to assign a follow-up activity based on the list generated during the Roundtable.

3. If you follow the same procedure orally, it is called Round Robin.

Numbered Heads Together

Step-by-Step

Step 1. Teacher plans for type of responses

    a. For example:

        1. Black/Enamel Board Response—Designate a section of the board for each team

        2. Slate Response—Give each team a small slate, chalk, or enamel board

        3. Choral Response—Each team reporter calls out the answer

        4. Random Call/Individual Responds—The teacher randomly selects a team reporter or student to respond

Step 2. Team members number off

    a. On each team, each person takes a different number. The first person is person #1; the second is person #2, and so on.

Step 3. Teacher poses a question

Step 4. Teams put heads together and decide on their answer

Step 5. Teacher calls time

    a. Team discussion stops

Step 6. Teacher randomly selects a number

    a. The teacher can use a spinner, a deck of number cards, a deck of cards with team names, a deck of cards with student names, or any other random technique.

Step 7. Those students whose number is selected stand, i.e. number 1, 2, 3, or 4.

    a. Use the response technique as selected by the teacher in step 1 to have students respond.

    b. The teacher then randomly calls on a table. The group member from that table who is standing gives an answer.

    c. The other group members who are standing agree or disagree with answer.

    d. This can be done with a disagree/agree card or by voting thumbs up or down.

Step 8. Repeat process

    a. Repeat steps 3—7 until all questions are answered.

You may give points for each correct answer and calculate quiz grades for team members if you wish. The authors rarely use this option.

Building a T-Chart

A very effective method of defining a social skill is to develop a T-chart for it. Use the steps below to construct your chart.

1. Write the name of the skill to be learned and practiced at the top of the chart and draw a large T below it.
2. Label the left side of the T *Looks Like* and the right side *Sounds Like*.
3. Think of an example for each of the columns and write that below the crossbar.
4. Ask for other behaviors that operationalize the skill (looks like) and list those on the left side.
5. Ask for further phrases that operationalize the skill (sounds like) and list those on the right side.
6. Have group members practice both *Looks Like* and *Sounds Like* before the lesson is concluded.
7. See the next page for an actual example.

Social Skill

(for example, equal participation)

Looks Like	Sounds Like

Sample T-Chart

One teacher had cooperative teams generate T-chart posters on ways they disagreed in agreeable ways after discussing a multi-faceted issue. Items could and should be added to each poster in subsequent lessons. A sample poster might be as follows:

Disagreeing in an Agreeable Way

Looks Like	Sounds Like
1. Eye contact with subtle shake of the head	1. I understand what you are saying . . . we might also want to consider . . . ."
2. Smiling while you make your statement	2. "I see your point, however . . .
3. Group members listening fully to one another's ideas before commenting	3. "Your point is important, but I wonder if another idea might be . . ."
4. Slight shoulder shrug and head shake	4. "I don't agree because . . ."
5. Etc.	5. "That's an interesting idea, nonetheless . . ."
	6. You may want to consider . . ."
	7. Etc.

Using Questions to Identify Levels of Comprehension

Teachers can identify the level of comprehension (Reid, 1983, 1997a, 1997b) of a question by using the following definitions and answering the related questions. It is good practice not only to be able to identify the level of comprehension of a question but to be able to ask questions on all four levels during discussions and individual conferences. Studies looking at the levels of comprehension of questions asked in classrooms and in textbooks indicate that most questions are literal with not much variation in level. If we want our students to think creatively and critically, we need to be able to ask questions that require those kinds of thought patterns in order to answer.

1. Literal
    a. The answer to the question is stated directly (word for word) in the text or the speech. What are the four levels of questions that can be used to determine students' comprehension or understanding of the material? is an example.

2. Interpretive
    a. The answer to the question is not directly stated in the material but enough detail is given so that the answer makes sense. Is the answer based upon details in the material but not directly stated? What details in the material give you that idea? is a question you should ask to verify whether the inference or generalization is warranted.

3. Critical
    a. The reader/listener makes judgments about the accuracy of the information, identifies fiction, and identifies and analyzes propaganda. Is judgment about accuracy or truth asked for? Is fact or truth in question?

4. Creative
    a. The reader/listener involves herself/himself in the material or extends the material. Does the question ask for something new to be created? What would you have done if you were in his/her place? is an example. What do you think happened before this, or after this? is another example.

Asking Questions

"What's in a question, you ask? Everything. It is the way of evoking stimulating response or stultifying inquiry. It is the essence, the very core of teaching." (Dewey, J. 1933)

There is nothing more evident that teachers do, other than lecture, than ask questions. It is what teachers do. Some scholars have reported that teachers ask several hundred questions per day. Gall (1970) reported an average of 395 questions a day asked by teachers. Calculated for a year teachers ask around 70,000 questions and 1.5 million in a typical career. In considering basic moves of teaching, nothing is more basic to the teaching process than asking questions. It also is directly related to our definition of teaching—getting responses from students in an organized, systematic manner.

Asking questions also assumes great importance because it determines what students learn. What teachers ask about and how they ask determines, to a great extent, what students believe is important. Questions can stimulate either simple or complex thought patterns—"Questions establish the level of cognitive activity on the part of the listener . . ." (Wiles and Bondi, 2005).

There are, in spite of what is available to guide our practice in writing and asking questions, a number of problems associated with the process of asking questions and getting students to answer. You will readily recognize them. They are listed below.

1. Students often do not want to answer.
2. Extroverted students and those considered more capable are called on to answer questions much more often than students who are introverted or considered less capable.
3. Most questions are literal, lower level, and call for convergent thinking rather than interpretive and divergent thinking. "Research since 1970 shows that most teachers' questions (50,000 per year) are didactic or procedural and often produce listlessness in students" (Wiles & Bondi, 2005).
4. Higher order thinking processes are not promoted by questions teachers ask. Seventy to ninety-five percent of the questions teachers ask do not require deep thinking (Gall, & Rhody, 1987).
5. Students are reluctant to answer questions requiring higher order thinking processes.

6. Teachers often do not allow enough time for students to answer questions particularly questions requiring higher order thinking; the average time a teacher waits is less than one second (Rowe, 1986).

Have you ever made a presentation and asked for an answer to a question and no one volunteered? Or have you been dissatisfied with the depth of an answer? Do the same students tend to want to answer each time you ask a question?

Most, if not all, of us have experienced these problems, often on a daily basis. It is a persistent problem. Sadker and Sadker (1999) sum it up this way: "Research studies indicate that classroom questions play a crucial role in the classroom and that teachers need to improve their questioning practices." Thankfully, the solutions to these problems are relatively easy to put into place. We will detail the basic moves of asking questions and getting responses below.

What Would a Typical Lesson Look Like?

There are, happily, ways to alleviate the problems listed above. There are five steps. The basic moves (steps) in questioning are these:

1. Teacher poses a question. Use one of the frameworks (convergent/divergent; 4 levels of questions; Bloom's Taxonomy) to guide the level of questions asked.
2. Teacher gives students time to think (three seconds to several minutes is appropriate depending upon question asked).
3. Students discuss their answers with their peers. Use one of the structures, that is, Turn-to-Your-Neighbor, if teaching an informal cooperative learning lesson or Pair-Square, Round Robin, Rally Table, and so forth, if teaching a formal cooperative learning lesson.
4. Teacher calls on students to respond. The most frequently used response structure is to call on students randomly by the use of Random Call cards. If teaching a formal cooperative learning lesson, the reporter from the group could also report.
5. Teacher opens the floor for volunteers after 2-6 participants are randomly called on (participants raise their hands to be recognized by the teacher).

The short version is:

1. Teacher poses a question
2. Teacher asks students to think silently
3. Students, after a set time, discuss their answer with a peer and/or peer group
4. Teacher calls on students randomly to share with the class
5. Teacher opens the floor for volunteers to respond

It is relatively easy to learn to use this process. You will become much more adept at getting responses from your students. Remember our definition of teaching: teaching is getting responses from learners in an organized, systematic manner. Using this simple process will enable you to become a much more effective teacher.

People Hunt

A Class Building Activity

Find someone who	Name
Can list 6 character traits we have studied	
Can define patience	
Is able to name their favorite character trait	
Can repeat the text for perseverance	
Knows the definition for obedience	
Can define character	
Can tell which character trait Ecclesiastes 9:10 refers to	
Can define perseverance	
Is able to find a story that illustrates efficiency in the Bible	
Can repeat James 1:19	
Can identify the only thing we can take to heaven	
Can repeat the text that encourages us to be patient	
Can define kindness	
Can identify another word for listen	
Can repeat Philippians 4:8	
Can name 4 cooperative structures	
Can define honesty	
Is able to tell how the character traits have helped them	
Can tell a word that means to continue to do something in spite of difficulties or obstacles	
Can identify a favorite character development story/activity and can give 2 reasons why it is their favorite	

Directions for using People Hunt/Find Someone Who Activity

1. Each person needs a copy of the People Hunt and a pen, or pencil.
   a. As far as the students are concerned, the objective is to see who can get the most statements signed before time is called. As far as the teacher is concerned the objective is for the students to review the information.
2. When given the signal all students stand up.
3. The students have to find other students who can do what the statement says. The students have to actually do what the statements say, they cannot just say, "Yes, I know it or yes, I can define kindness." For example, they must define kindness.
4. When students are able to perform the activity, the student who asked the question writes the name of the student who responded next to the statement.
   a. Be sure they write legibly so they can identify the person later.
5. If you have 20 or more students, each student is required to get 20 different signatures.
   a. If you have 10 students, each student can only sign the paper twice.
   b. If you have 5 students, each student can sign the paper four times, etc.
6. When time is up, each person returns to their seat and you have them report.

There are different ways to have them report. One way is to begin by asking, "Who answered question number 1?" Call on one of the students. For example, "Okay, Jake, who was able to name the 6 traits we have studied so far? He may say, Todd." You may have Todd repeat what he said, or you may have Jake repeat what Todd said. Then you ask Todd, "Who answered number 2 for you?" Continue until you reach number 20. The kids enjoy this and it is a fun way to review. You can change the questions and use this activity in any subject area.

A List of Character Traits

Listed below are character traits gathered from a number of different sources and compiled for your information and possible use.

1. Appreciation	32. Love
2. Attentiveness	33. Loyalty
3. Availability	34. Obedience
4. Commitment	35. Patience
5. Compassion	36. Peacefulness
6. Confidence	37. Resourcefulness
7. Consideration	38. Responsibility
8. Consistency	39. Reverence
9. Contentment	40. Self-control
10. Cooperation	41. Temperance
11. Courage	42. Tenderheartedness
12. Creativity	43. Thankfulness
13. Decisiveness	44. Tolerance
14. Dependability	45. Truthfulness
15. Determination	46. Understanding
16. Diligence	47. Wisdom
17. Discernment	48. Worship
18. Efficiency	
19. Fairness	
20. Faithfulness	
21. Fearlessness	
22. Flexibility	
23. Forgiveness	
24. Friendliness	
25. Generosity	
26. Gentleness	
27. Helpfulness	
28. Honesty	
29. Humbleness	
30. Joyfulness	
31. Kindness	

References

Coriell, Ron & Rebekah, (2008). *A child's book of character building—Book 1.* Grand Rapids, MI: Fleming H. Revell.

Engen, Sadie Owen, (1980). *Living and learning: Worship stories for young children.* Washington, D.C.: Review and Herald Publishing Association.

Green, William H., & Henriquez-Green, Rita (2008). *Basic moves of teaching: Building on cooperative learning.* Victoria, BC, Canada: Trafford Publishing.

Irland, Nancy Beck & Peter Beck, (1989). *Daily devotionals: Out of this world.* Haggerstown, MD: Review and Herald Publishing Association.

Kuzma, Kay, (1989). *Building your child's character from the inside out.* Elgin, IL: David C. Cook Publishing.

Maxwell, Arthur S., (1951). *Uncle Arthur's bedtime stories.* Washington, D.C.: Review and Herald Publishing Association.

Rasmussen, Bernard Ingram, (1979). *Character craft, per se: A source book in moral education.* Angwin, CA: The Dupli-Craft Company, Publishers.

Stubbs, Betty, (1954). *Bible object lessons for boys and girls.* Cincinnati, OH: The Standard Publishing Company.

AVAILABLE FROM THE ADVENTIST BOOK CENTER (1-800-765-6955)

Your Story Hour Adventures in Life: Albums 8-11 are character development stories. They have new materials too. 1-800-987-7879 http://www.yourstoryhour.org/

My Bible Friends DVD is available through the Review & Herald Publishing Association.

All the stories are on one DVD which costs $19.95. http://www.reviewandherald.com/index. php/products/books.rhpa

Uncle Arthur's Bedtime Stories books are still available at http://www.uncle-arthurs.com/ua/ browse_books.php?search=1&search_terms=bedtime+stor

The audio is no longer available. That may be a great project for some of your better students to do some research and find copies or to produce themselves.